A TESTIMONY of JESUS

Writings of Solomon

JIMMIE JENNINGS

Copyright © 2020 by Jimmie Jennings.

ISBN Softcover 978-1-951469-73-3

Scripture references are from the e-Sword King James Version (KJV) of the Bible.

Illustrations and figures were taken from the Internet and Encyclopedia references.

All rights reserved. No part of this book may be reproduced or transmitted in any form or by any means, electronic or mechanical, including photocopying, recording, or by any information storage and retrieval system without express written permission from the author, except in the case of brief quotations embodied in critical reviews and certain other non-commercial uses permitted by copyright law.

Printed in the United States of America.

To order additional copies of this book, contact:
Bookwhip
1-855-339-3589
https://www.bookwhip.com

CONTENTS

Preface 1

Introduction 3

Proverbs 5

    Proverbs 1 through 9: "Proverbs of Solomon, Son of David" 5
        The Value of proverbs 5
        Advice to Young Men 5
        The Rewards of Wisdom 7
        More Advice 8
        The Benefits of Wisdom 10
        Warning Against Sexual Sin 12
        Warning Against Idleness & Falsehood 13
        Warning Against Adultery 14
        A Prostitute's Trap 15
        Wisdom 17
        Wisdom And the Foolish Woman 19

    Proverbs 10 through 22:16: "Some Other Proverbs of Solomon" ... 20
        Proverbs 10 20
        Proverbs 11 22
        Proverbs 12 24
        Proverbs 13 26
        Proverbs 14 27
        Proverbs 15 29
        Proverbs 16 31
        Proverbs 17 33
        Proverbs 18 35
        Proverbs 19 37
        Proverbs 20 38

  Proverbs 21 40
  Proverbs 22 through 22:16 42

Proverbs 22:17 through 24:34: "The Sayings of the Wise" 43
  More Wise Sayings 43
  Proverbs 23 44
  Proverbs 24 46
  Proverbs 24:1 through 24:22 46
  Proverbs 24:23 through 24:34 47

Proverbs 25 through 29:27: "More Proverbs of Solomon that
 the Councilors of King Hezekiah of Judah Compiled" 48
  Proverbs 25 48
  Proverbs 26 50
  Proverbs 27 52
  Proverbs 28 53
  Proverbs 29 55

 Proverbs 30 and 31 57

 Proverbs 30: "The Words of Agur" 57

 Proverbs 31:1 through 31:9: "The Words of King Lemuel of
  Massa, Which his Mother Taught Him" 59

 Proverb 31:10 through 31: The ideal wise woman (elsewhere
  called "the woman of substance") 59

Songs of Songs, Or Songs of Solomon 62
 The First Song 64
 The Second Song 66
 The Third Song 67
 The Fouth Song 69
 The Fifth Song 71
 The Sixth Song 73

Ecclesiastes 75
 The LORD God Established Cycles of Events in His Creation ... 77
 Ecclesiastes Chapter 1 78

  Solomon did not Always Consult the LORD God 80
 Ecclesiastes Chapter 2 81
  But is There Any Gain from Labor Absent of the
   LORD God? 83
 Ecclesiastes Chapter 3 83
  A Season and Time for Every Purpose Under Heaven 83
  It Seems Solomon Did Not have the Full
   Revelation of Salvation? 85
 Ecclesiastes Chapter 4 92
  What Help is There for the Oppressed Without A
   Comforter 92
 Ecclesiastes Chapter 5 94
  Being Mindful of Right Behavior before the
   LORD God 94
 Ecclesiastes Chapter 6 95
  Everyone Seeks to Enjoy the Gains from Their Labor 95
 Ecclesiastes Chapter 7 97
  There are Obstacles to Gaining a Good Reputation 97
 Ecclesiastes Chapter 8 99
 Ecclesiastes Chapter 9 100
  The LORD God Has Subjected All to the Same
   "Whosoever Requirements" 100
 Ecclesiastes Chapter 10 102
 Ecclesiastes Chapter 11 104
 Ecclesiastes Chapter 12 105
 A Summary of Ecclesiastes 106

Book Summary 111
 God Uses Whomsoever, According to His Purpose 111
 Reconciliations unto the Atonement 123

Definitions & Figures 143

Previous Writings 181

PREFACE

The Holy Spirit Inspired King Solomon and several Others' at various times in these Judeo – Christian Bible Texts, unto True Wisdom; which is the Knowledge of the LORD God of Creation!

These Expressions Also Addresses Issues in the Context of Every Generation's Day-to-Day Living; Natural, as well as Spiritual!

King Solomon wrote more of the **Proverbs** in the *Book of the Proverbs* than any other single servant of the LORD God! He also wrote, *"Songs of Solomon,* and the *Book of Ecclesiastes"*. A Search of reference material yielded the following:

We see that King Solomon followed the instruction of Moses in Deuteronomy 17:18; maybe without having realized, he the King, was expected to write a copy of his own Bible texts based upon the Law(s) of Moses; recorded the books that were with the Priesthood, and Levites in the Tabernacle, and Temple?

We know that King David also did this with his writings of the Psalms in his time of ruling Israel, before Solomon!

Also, for additional background, refer to, "Apocrypha Books" in the "Definitions & Figures" section.

One of the most important and well known <u>themes</u> *King Solomon declares in the* **Proverbs** *may have already been introduced by his father King David, or even some others before David; certainly it was not foreign to Moses! And that is the* <u>theme</u> *of "Wisdom"; See the following:*

Psa 111:10 The fear of the LORD *is* the beginning of wisdom: a good understanding have all they that do *his commandments:* his praise endureth for ever.

Pro 1:7 The fear of the LORD *is* the beginning of knowledge: *but* fools despise wisdom and instruction.

Pro 9:10 The fear of the LORD *is* the beginning of wisdom: and the knowledge of the holy *is* understanding.

Exo 28:3 And thou shalt speak unto all *that are* wise hearted, whom I have filled with the spirit of wisdom, that they may make Aaron's garments to consecrate him, that he may minister unto me in the priest's office.

Exo 31:3 And I have filled him with the spirit of God, in wisdom, and in understanding, and in knowledge, and in all manner of workmanship,

Exo 31:6 And I, behold, I have given with him Aholiab, the son of Ahisamach, of the tribe of Dan: and in the hearts of all that are wise hearted I have put wisdom, that they may make all that I have commanded thee;

Exo 35:26 And all the women whose heart stirred them up in wisdom spun goats' *hair.*

Exo 35:31 And he hath filled him with the spirit of God, in wisdom, in understanding, and in knowledge, and in all manner of workmanship;

INTRODUCTION

Old Testament Scriptures spoke the following about the Wisdom of Solomon:

1Ki 4:29 And God gave Solomon wisdom and understanding exceeding much, and largeness of heart, even as the sand that *is* on the sea shore.

1Ki 4:30 And Solomon's wisdom excelled the wisdom of all the children of the east country, and all the wisdom of Egypt.

1Ki 4:31 For he was wiser than all men ***(of his generation?)***; than Ethan the Ezrahite, and Heman, and Chalcol, and Darda, the sons of Mahol: and his fame was in all nations round about.

1Ki 4:32 And he spake three thousand ***(3,000)*** proverbs: and his songs were a thousand and five ***(1,005)***.

1Ki 4:33 And he spake of trees, from the cedar tree that *is* in Lebanon even unto the hyssop that springeth out of the wall: he spake also of beasts, and of fowl, and of creeping things, and of fishes.

1Ki 4:34 And there came of all people to hear the wisdom of Solomon, from all kings of the earth, which had heard of his wisdom.

Also, New Testament Scripture says the following of "Wisdom":

Jas 1:17 Every good gift and every perfect gift is from above, and cometh down from the Father of lights, with whom is no variableness, neither shadow of turning.

Jas 3:13 Who *is* a wise man and endued with knowledge among you? let him shew out of a good conversation his works with meekness ***(or without boasting)*** of ***(his)*** wisdom.

Jas 3:14 But if ye have bitter envying and strife in your hearts, glory not, and lie not against the truth.

Jas 3:15 This wisdom *(of Jas 3:14)* descendeth not from above, but *is* earthly, sensual, devilish.

Jas 3:16 For where envying and strife *is*, there *is* confusion and every evil work.

Jas 3:17 But the wisdom that is from above is first pure, then peaceable, gentle, *and* easy to be intreated *(asked, or demanded of?)*, full of mercy and good fruits, without partiality *(or favoritism)*, and without hypocrisy *(pretense; deceit)*.

In addition to being inspirational; giving praise and credit unto God, a great many of these texts are also prophetic; thus, pointing to the Lord Jesus Christ, often; even unto end time events and then eternity?

PROVERBS

Proverbs 1 through 9: "Proverbs of Solomon, Son of David"

Proverbs 1
The Value of proverbs
Pro 1:1 The proverbs of Solomon the son of David, king of Israel;
Pro 1:2 To know wisdom and instruction; to perceive the words of understanding;
Pro 1:3 To receive the instruction of wisdom, justice, and judgment, and equity;
Pro 1:4 To give subtilty to the simple, to the young man knowledge and discretion.
Pro 1:5 A wise *man* will hear, and will increase learning; and a man of understanding shall attain unto *(or look for)* wise counsels:
Pro 1:6 To understand a proverb, and the interpretation; the words of the wise, and their dark *(or hidden)* sayings.

Advice to Young Men
Pro 1:7 The fear of the LORD *is* the beginning of knowledge: *but* fools despise wisdom and instruction.
Pro 1:8 My son, hear the instruction of thy father, and forsake not the law of thy mother:
Pro 1:9 For they *shall be* an ornament of grace unto thy head, and chains about thy neck.

Pro 1:10 My son, if sinners entice thee, consent *(or agree)* thou not.
Pro 1:11 If they *(sinners)* say, Come with us, let us lay wait for blood, let us lurk privily for the innocent without cause:
Pro 1:12 Let us swallow them *(the innocent)* up alive as the grave; and whole, as those that go down into the pit:

Pro 1:13 We shall find all precious substance, we shall fill our houses with spoil:

Pro 1:14 Cast in thy lot among us; let us all have one purse:

Pro 1:15 My son, walk not thou in the way with them *(sinners)*; refrain thy foot from their path:

Pro 1:16 For their *(the sinners)* feet run to evil, and make haste to shed blood.

Pro 1:17 Surely in vain the net is spread in the sight of any bird ***(unless the net is (hidden, or disguised), efforts to capture the bird is in vain)***.

Pro 1:18 And they lay wait for their *own* blood; they lurk privily for their *own* lives.

Pro 1:19 So *are* the ways of every one that is greedy of gain; *which* taketh away the life of the owners thereof.

Pro 1:20 Wisdom crieth without; she uttereth her voice in the streets:

Pro 1:21 She crieth in the chief place of concourse, in the openings of the gates: in the city she uttereth her words, *saying,*

Pro 1:22 How long, ye simple ones, will ye love simplicity? and the scorners delight in their scorning, and fools hate knowledge?

Pro 1:23 Turn you at my reproof: behold, I will pour out my spirit unto you, I will make known my words unto you.

Pro 1:24 Because I have called, and ye refused; I have stretched out my hand, and no man regarded;

Pro 1:25 But ye have set at nought all my counsel, and would *(accept)* none of my reproof *(or correction)*:

Pro 1:26 I also will laugh at your calamity; I will mock when your fear cometh;

Pro 1:27 When your fear cometh as desolation, and your destruction cometh as a whirlwind; when distress and anguish cometh upon you.

Pro 1:28 Then shall they call upon me, but I will not answer; they shall seek me early, but they shall not find me:

Pro 1:29 For that they hated knowledge, and did not choose the fear of the LORD:

Pro 1:30 They would *(accept)* none of my counsel: they despised all my reproof *(or correction)*.

Pro 1:31 Therefore shall they eat of the fruit of their own way, and be filled with their own devices.

Pro 1:32 For the turning away of the simple shall slay them, and the prosperity of fools shall destroy them.

Pro 1:33 But whoso hearkeneth unto me shall dwell safely, and shall be quiet from fear of evil.

Proverbs 2
The Rewards of Wisdom

Pro 2:1 My son, if thou wilt receive my words, and hide my commandments with thee;

Pro 2:2 So that thou incline thine ear unto wisdom, *and* apply thine heart to understanding;

Pro 2:3 Yea, if thou criest after knowledge, *and* liftest up thy voice for understanding;

Pro 2:4 If thou seekest her *(knowledge, understanding, wisdom)* as silver, and searchest for her as *for* hid treasures;

Pro 2:5 Then shalt thou understand the fear *(and respect)* of the LORD, and find the knowledge of God.

Pro 2:6 For the LORD giveth wisdom: out of his mouth *cometh* knowledge and understanding.

Pro 2:7 He layeth up sound wisdom for the righteous: *he is* a buckler *(or shield)* to them that walk uprightly.

Pro 2:8 He keepeth the paths of judgment *(or that which is right)*, and preserveth the way of his saints.

Pro 2:9 Then shalt thou understand righteousness, and judgment, and equity; *yea,* every good path.

Pro 2:10 When wisdom entereth into thine heart, and knowledge is pleasant unto thy soul;

Pro 2:11 Discretion *(or common sense)* shall preserve thee, understanding shall keep thee:

Pro 2:12 To deliver thee from the way of the evil *man,* from the man that speaketh froward *(or contrary)* things;

Pro 2:13 Who leave the paths of uprightness, to walk in the ways of darkness;

Pro 2:14 Who rejoice to do evil, *and* delight in the frowardness of the wicked;

Pro 2:15 Whose ways *are* crooked, and *they* froward in their paths:

Pro 2:16 To deliver thee from the strange woman, *even* from the stranger *which* flattereth with her words;

Pro 2:17 Which forsaketh the guide of her youth, and forgetteth the covenant of her God.

Pro 2:18 For her house inclineth unto death, and her paths unto the dead.

Pro 2:19 None that go unto her return again, neither take they hold of the paths of life.

Pro 2:20 That thou mayest walk in the way of good *men*, and keep the paths of the righteous.

Pro 2:21 For the upright shall dwell in the land, and the perfect shall remain in it.

Pro 2:22 But the wicked shall be cut off from the earth, and the transgressors shall be rooted out of it **(the earth)**.

Proverbs 3

More Advice

Pro 3:1 My son, forget not my law; but let thine heart keep my commandments:

Pro 3:2 For length of days, and long life, and peace, shall they add to thee.

Pro 3:3 Let not mercy and truth forsake **(or abandon)** thee: bind **(mercy and truth)** them about thy neck; write them upon the table of thine heart:

Pro 3:4 So shalt thou find favour and good understanding in the sight of God and man.

Pro 3:5 Trust in the LORD with all thine heart; and lean not unto thine own understanding.

Pro 3:6 In all thy ways acknowledge him, and he shall direct thy paths.

Pro 3:7 Be not wise in thine own eyes: fear the LORD, and depart from evil.

Pro 3:8 It shall be health to thy navel, and marrow to thy bones.

Pro 3:9 Honour the LORD with thy substance, and with the firstfruits of all thine increase *(in other words, support the work of God)*:

Pro 3:10 So shall thy barns be filled with plenty, and thy presses shall burst out with new wine.

Pro 3:11 My son, despise not the chastening of the LORD; neither be weary of his correction:

Pro 3:12 For whom the LORD loveth he correcteth; even as a father the son *in whom* he delighteth.

Pro 3:13 Happy *is* the man *that* findeth wisdom, and the man *that* getteth understanding.

Pro 3:14 For the merchandise of it *is* better than the merchandise of silver, and the gain thereof than fine gold.

Pro 3:15 She *(wisdom) is* more precious than rubies: and all the things thou canst desire are not to be compared unto her *(wisdom)*.

Pro 3:16 Length of days *is* in her right hand; *and* in her left hand riches and honour.

Pro 3:17 Her ways *are* ways of pleasantness, and all her paths *are* peace.

Pro 3:18 She *(wisdom) is* a tree of life to them that lay hold upon her: and happy *is every one* that retaineth her.

Pro 3:19 The LORD by wisdom hath founded the earth; by understanding hath he established the heavens.

Pro 3:20 By his knowledge the depths are broken up, and the clouds drop down the dew.

Pro 3:21 My son, let not them *(wisdom, understanding, and knowledge)* depart from thine eyes: keep sound wisdom and discretion *(care)*:

Pro 3:22 So shall they *(wisdom, understanding, knowledge, and discretion\care)* be life unto thy soul, and grace to thy neck.

Pro 3:23 Then shalt thou walk in thy way safely, and thy foot shall not stumble.

Pro 3:24 When thou liest down, thou shalt not be afraid: yea, thou shalt lie down, and thy sleep shall be sweet.

Pro 3:25 Be not afraid of sudden fear, neither of the desolation of the wicked, when it cometh.

Pro 3:26 For the LORD shall be thy confidence, and shall keep thy foot from being taken.

Pro 3:27 Withhold not good from them to whom it is due, when it is in the power of thine hand to do *it*.

Pro 3:28 Say not unto thy neighbour, Go, and come again, and to morrow I will give; when thou hast it by thee.

Pro 3:29 Devise not evil against thy neighbour, seeing he dwelleth securely by thee.

Pro 3:30 Strive not with a man without cause, if he have done thee no harm.

Pro 3:31 Envy thou not the oppressor, and choose none of his ways.

Pro 3:32 For the froward *(contrary) is* abomination to the LORD: but his secret *is* with the righteous.

Pro 3:33 The curse of the LORD *is* in the house of the wicked: but he blesseth the habitation of the just.

Pro 3:34 Surely he scorneth the scorners: but he giveth grace unto the lowly.

Pro 3:35 The wise shall inherit glory: but shame shall be the promotion of fools.

Proverbs 4

The Benefits of Wisdom

Pro 4:1 Hear, ye children, the instruction of a father, and attend to know understanding.

Pro 4:2 For I give you good doctrine, forsake ye not my law.

Pro 4:3 For I was my father's son, tender and only *beloved* in the sight of my mother.

Pro 4:4 He taught me also, and said unto me, Let thine heart retain my words: keep my commandments, and live.

Pro 4:5 Get wisdom, get understanding: forget *it* not; neither decline from the words of my mouth.

Pro 4:6 Forsake her not, and she shall preserve thee: love her, and she shall keep thee.

Pro 4:7 Wisdom *is* the principal thing; *therefore* get wisdom: and with all thy getting get understanding.

Pro 4:8 Exalt her, and she shall promote thee: she shall bring thee to honour, when thou dost embrace her.

Pro 4:9 She shall give to thine head an ornament of grace: a crown of glory shall she deliver to thee.

Pro 4:10 Hear, O my son, and receive my sayings; and the years of thy life shall be many.

Pro 4:11 I have taught thee in the way of wisdom; I have led thee in right paths.

Pro 4:12 When thou goest, thy steps shall not be straitened; and when thou runnest, thou shalt not stumble.

Pro 4:13 Take fast hold of instruction; let *her* not go: keep her; for she *is* thy life.

Pro 4:14 Enter not into the path of the wicked, and go not in the way of evil *men*.

Pro 4:15 Avoid it, pass not by it, turn from it, and pass away.

Pro 4:16 For they sleep not, except they have done mischief; and their sleep is taken away, unless they cause *some* to fall.

Pro 4:17 For they eat the bread of wickedness, and drink the wine of violence.

Pro 4:18 But the path of the just *is* as the shining light, that shineth more and more unto the perfect day.

Pro 4:19 The way of the wicked *is* as darkness: they know not at what they stumble.

Pro 4:20 My son, attend to my words; incline thine ear unto my sayings.

Pro 4:21 Let them not depart from thine eyes; keep them in the midst of thine heart.

Pro 4:22 For they *are* life unto those that find them, and health to all their flesh.

Pro 4:23 Keep thy heart with all diligence; for out of it *are* the issues of life.

Pro 4:24 Put away from thee a froward mouth, and perverse lips put far from thee.

Pro 4:25 Let thine eyes look right on, and let thine eyelids look straight before thee.

Pro 4:26 Ponder the path of thy feet, and let all thy ways be established.

Pro 4:27 Turn not to the right hand nor to the left: remove thy foot from evil.

Proverbs 5
Warning Against Sexual Sin

Pro 5:1 My son, attend unto my wisdom, *and* bow thine ear to my understanding:

Pro 5:2 That thou mayest regard discretion *(or proceed with careful, sober action)*, and *that* thy lips may keep knowledge.

Pro 5:3 For the lips of a strange woman drop *as* an honeycomb, and her mouth *is* smoother than oil:

Pro 5:4 But her end is bitter as wormwood, sharp as a twoedged sword.

Pro 5:5 Her feet go down to death; her steps take hold on hell.

Pro 5:6 Lest thou shouldest ponder the path of life, her ways are moveable, *that* thou canst not know *them*.

Pro 5:7 Hear me now therefore, O ye children, and depart not from the words of my mouth.

Pro 5:8 Remove thy way far from her, and come not nigh the door of her house:

Pro 5:9 Lest thou give thine honour unto others, and thy years unto the cruel:

Pro 5:10 Lest strangers be filled with thy wealth; and thy labours *be* in the house of a stranger *(we can certainly view times in history when men's wealth and labors became possessions of strangers (i.e., be in the house of a stranger))*;

Pro 5:11 And thou mourn at the last, when thy flesh and thy body are consumed,

Pro 5:12 And say, How have I hated instruction, and my heart despised reproof;

Pro 5:13 And have not obeyed the voice of my teachers, nor inclined mine ear to them that instructed me!

Pro 5:14 I was almost in all evil in the midst of the congregation and assembly.
Pro 5:15 Drink waters out of thine own cistern, and running waters out of thine own well.
Pro 5:16 Let thy fountains be dispersed abroad, *and* rivers of waters in the streets.
Pro 5:17 Let them be only thine own, and not strangers' with thee.
Pro 5:18 Let thy fountain be blessed: and rejoice with the wife of thy youth.
Pro 5:19 *Let her be as* the loving hind and pleasant roe; let her breasts satisfy thee at all times; and be thou ravished always with her love.
Pro 5:20 And why wilt thou, my son, be ravished with a strange woman, and embrace the bosom of a stranger?
Pro 5:21 For the ways of man *are* before the eyes of the LORD, and he pondereth all his goings.
Pro 5:22 His own iniquities shall take the wicked himself, and he shall be holden with the cords of his sins.
Pro 5:23 He shall die without instruction; and in the greatness of his folly he shall go astray.

Proverbs 6
Warning Against Idleness & Falsehood
Pro 6:1 My son, if thou be surety *(guarantee, or co-signed)* for thy friend, *if* thou hast stricken thy hand with a stranger,
Pro 6:2 Thou art snared with the words of thy mouth, thou art taken with the words of thy mouth.
Pro 6:3 Do this now, my son, and deliver thyself, when thou art come into the hand of thy friend; go, humble thyself, and make sure thy friend *(is a friend)*.

Pro 6:4 Give not sleep to thine eyes, nor slumber to thine eyelids.
Pro 6:5 Deliver thyself as a roe from the hand *of the hunter,* and as a bird from the hand of the fowler.
Pro 6:6 Go to the ant, thou sluggard; consider her ways, and be wise:
Pro 6:7 Which having no guide, overseer, or ruler,

Pro 6:8 Provideth her meat in the summer, *and* gathereth her food in the harvest.
Pro 6:9 How long wilt thou sleep, O sluggard? when wilt thou arise out of thy sleep?
Pro 6:10 *Yet* a little sleep, a little slumber, a little folding of the hands to sleep:
Pro 6:11 So shall thy poverty come as one that travelleth, and thy want as an armed man.

Pro 6:12 A naughty person, a wicked man, walketh with a froward mouth.
Pro 6:13 He winketh with his eyes, he speaketh with his feet, he teacheth with his fingers;
Pro 6:14 Frowardness *is* in his heart, he deviseth mischief continually; he soweth discord.
Pro 6:15 Therefore shall his calamity come suddenly; suddenly shall he be broken without remedy.

Pro 6:16 These six *things* doth the LORD hate: yea, seven *are* an abomination unto him:
Pro 6:17 A proud look, a lying tongue, and hands that shed innocent blood,
Pro 6:18 An heart that deviseth wicked imaginations, feet that be swift in running to mischief,
Pro 6:19 A false witness *that* speaketh lies, and he that soweth discord among brethren.

Warning Against Adultery
Pro 6:20 My son, keep thy father's commandment, and forsake not the law of thy mother:
Pro 6:21 Bind them continually upon thine heart, *and* tie them about thy neck.
Pro 6:22 When thou goest, it shall lead thee; when thou sleepest, it shall keep thee; and *when* thou awakest, it shall talk with thee.

Pro 6:23 For the commandment *is* a lamp; and the law *is* light; and reproofs of instruction *are* the way of life:

Pro 6:24 To keep thee from the evil woman, from the flattery of the tongue of a strange woman.

Pro 6:25 Lust not after her beauty in thine heart; neither let her take thee with her eyelids.

Pro 6:26 For by means of a whorish woman *a man is brought* to a piece of bread: and the adulteress will hunt for the precious life.

Pro 6:27 Can a man take fire in his bosom, and his clothes not be burned?

Pro 6:28 Can one go upon hot coals, and his feet not be burned?

Pro 6:29 So he that goeth in to his neighbour's wife; whosoever toucheth her shall not be innocent.

Pro 6:30 *Men* do not despise a thief, if he steal to satisfy his soul when he is hungry;

Pro 6:31 But *if* he be found, he shall restore sevenfold; he shall give all the substance of his house.

Pro 6:32 *But* whoso committeth adultery with a woman lacketh understanding: he *that* doeth it destroyeth his own soul.

Pro 6:33 A wound and dishonour shall he get; and his reproach shall not be wiped away.

Pro 6:34 For jealousy *is* the rage of a man: therefore he will not spare in the day of vengeance.

Pro 6:35 He will not regard any ransom; neither will he rest content, though thou givest many gifts.

Proverbs 7

A Prostitute's Trap

Pro 7:1 My son, keep my words, and lay up my commandments with thee.

Pro 7:2 Keep my commandments, and live; and my law as the apple of thine eye.

Pro 7:3 Bind them upon thy fingers, write them upon the table of thine heart.

Pro 7:4 Say unto wisdom, Thou *art* my sister; and call understanding *thy* kinswoman:

Pro 7:5 That they may keep thee from the strange woman, from the stranger *which* flattereth with her words.

Pro 7:6 For at the window of my house I looked through my casement,

Pro 7:7 And beheld among the simple ones, I discerned among the youths, a young man void of understanding,

Pro 7:8 Passing through the street near her corner; and he went the way to her house,

Pro 7:9 In the twilight, in the evening, in the black and dark night:

Pro 7:10 And, behold, there met him a woman *with* the attire of an harlot, and subtil *(or elusive)* of heart.

Pro 7:11 (She *is* loud and stubborn; her feet abide not in her house:

Pro 7:12 Now *is she* without, now in the streets, and lieth in wait at every corner.)

Pro 7:13 So she caught him, and kissed him, *and* with an impudent face said unto him,

Pro 7:14 *I have* peace offerings with me; this day have I payed my vows.

Pro 7:15 Therefore came I forth to meet thee, diligently to seek thy face, and I have found thee.

Pro 7:16 I have decked my bed with coverings of tapestry, with carved *works*, with fine linen of Egypt.

Pro 7:17 I have perfumed my bed with myrrh *(or incense)*, aloes, and cinnamon.

Pro 7:18 Come, let us take our fill of love until the morning: let us solace *(or enjoy)* ourselves with loves *(making?)*.

Pro 7:19 For the goodman *is* not at home, he is gone a long journey:

Pro 7:20 He hath taken a bag of money with him, *and* will come home at the day appointed.

Pro 7:21 With her much fair speech she caused him to yield, with the flattering of her lips she forced him.

Pro 7:22 He goeth after her straightway, as an ox goeth to the slaughter, or as a fool to the correction of the stocks;

Pro 7:23 Till a dart strike through his liver; as a bird hasteth to the snare, and knoweth not that it *is* for his life.

Pro 7:24 Hearken unto me now therefore, O ye children, and attend to the words of my mouth.

Pro 7:25 Let not thine heart decline to her ways, go not astray in her paths.

Pro 7:26 For she hath cast down many wounded: yea, many strong *men* have been slain by her.

Pro 7:27 Her house *is* the way to hell, going down to the chambers of death.

Proverbs 8
Wisdom

Pro 8:1 Doth not wisdom cry *(or yell out loud)*? and understanding put forth her voice *(and does not hide)*?

Pro 8:2 She *(understanding and wisdom)* standeth in the top of high places, by the way in the places of the paths *(of earth's citizens)*.

Pro 8:3 She *(understanding and wisdom)* crieth at the gates, at the entry of the city, at the coming in at the doors.

Pro 8:4 Unto you, O men, I call; and my voice *is* to the sons of man.

Pro 8:5 O ye simple, understand wisdom: and, ye fools, be ye of an understanding heart.

Pro 8:6 Hear; for I will speak of excellent things; and the opening of my lips *shall be* right things.

Pro 8:7 For my mouth shall speak truth; and wickedness *is* an abomination to my lips.

Pro 8:8 All the words of my mouth *are* in righteousness; *there is* nothing froward *(contrary)* or perverse in them *(the words of my mouth)*.

Pro 8:9 They *(the words of my mouth) are* all plain to him that understandeth, and right to them that find knowledge.

Pro 8:10 Receive my instruction, and not silver; and knowledge rather than choice gold.

Pro 8:11 For wisdom *is* better than rubies; and all the things that may be desired are not to be compared to it *(wisdom; the words of my mouth)*.

Pro 8:12 I wisdom dwell with prudence, and find out knowledge of witty *(or clever?)* inventions.

Wisdom, Fearing the LORD God; and when was there Wisdom!

Pro 8:13 The fear of the LORD *is* to hate evil: pride, and arrogancy, and the evil way, and the froward *(or contrary)* mouth, do I hate.

Pro 8:14 Counsel *is* mine, and sound wisdom: I *am* understanding; I have strength.

Pro 8:15 By me kings reign, and princes decree justice.

Pro 8:16 By me princes rule, and nobles, *even* all the judges of the earth.

Pro 8:17 I love them that love me; and those that seek me early shall find me.

Pro 8:18 Riches and honour *are* with me; *yea*, durable *(or long-lasting)* riches and righteousness.

Pro 8:19 My fruit *is* better than gold, yea, than fine gold; and my revenue *(or gain)* than choice silver.

Pro 8:20 I lead *(and go)* in the way of righteousness, in the midst of the paths of judgment:

Pro 8:21 That I may cause those that love me to inherit substance; and I will fill their treasures.

Pro 8:22 The LORD possessed me *(wisdom)* in the beginning of his way, before his works of old.

Pro 8:23 I *(wisdom)* was set up from everlasting, from the beginning, or ever the earth was.

Pro 8:24 When *there were* no depths, I *(wisdom)* was brought forth; when *there were* no fountains abounding with water.

Pro 8:25 Before the mountains were settled, before the hills was I *(wisdom)* brought forth:

Pro 8:26 While as yet he *(the LORD God)* had not made the earth, nor the fields, nor the highest part of the dust of the world.

Pro 8:27 When he prepared the heavens, I *(wisdom) was* there: when he set a compass upon the face of the depth:

Pro 8:28 When he established the clouds above: when he strengthened the fountains of the deep:

Pro 8:29 When he gave to the sea his decree, that the waters should not pass his commandment: when he appointed the foundations of the earth:

Pro 8:30 Then I *(wisdom)* was by him, *as* one brought up *with him:* and I was daily *his* delight, rejoicing always before him;

Pro 8:31 Rejoicing in the habitable part of his earth; and my delights *were* with the sons of men.

Pro 8:32 Now therefore hearken unto me, O ye children: for blessed *are they that* keep my ways *(the ways of God; the ways of Wisdom)*.

Pro 8:33 Hear instruction, and be wise, and refuse it not.

Pro 8:34 Blessed *is* the man that heareth me, watching daily at my gates, waiting at the posts of my doors.

Pro 8:35 For whoso findeth me findeth life, and shall obtain favour of the LORD.

Pro 8:36 But he that sinneth against me wrongeth his own soul: all they that hate me love death.

Proverbs 9
Wisdom And the Foolish Woman

Wisdom

Pro 9:1 Wisdom hath builded her house *(and reputation?)*, she hath hewn out her seven *(7)* pillars:

Pro 9:2 She hath killed her beasts; she hath mingled her wine; she hath also furnished her table.

Pro 9:3 She hath sent forth her maidens: she crieth upon the highest places of the city,

Pro 9:4 Whoso *is* simple, let him turn in hither: *as for* him that wanteth understanding, she saith to him,

Pro 9:5 Come, eat of my bread, and drink of the wine *which* I have mingled.

Pro 9:6 Forsake the foolish, and live; and go in the way of understanding.

Pro 9:7 He that reproveth a scorner getteth to himself shame: and he that rebuketh a wicked *man getteth* himself a blot.

Pro 9:8 Reprove not a scorner, lest he hate thee: rebuke a wise man, and he will love thee.

Pro 9:9 Give *instruction* to a wise *man,* and he will be yet wiser: teach a just *man,* and he will increase in learning.

Pro 9:10 The fear of the LORD *is* the beginning of wisdom: and the knowledge of the holy *is* understanding.

Pro 9:11 For by me thy days shall be multiplied, and the years of thy life shall be increased.

Pro 9:12 If thou be wise, thou shalt be wise for thyself: but *if* thou scornest, thou alone shalt bear *it*.

The Foolish Woman

Pro 9:13 A foolish woman *is* clamorous: *she is* simple, and knoweth nothing.

Pro 9:14 For she sitteth at the door of her house, on a seat in the high places of the city,

Pro 9:15 To call passengers who go right on their ways:

Pro 9:16 Whoso *is* simple, let him turn in hither: and *as for* him that wanteth understanding, she saith to him,

Pro 9:17 Stolen waters are sweet, and bread *eaten* in secret is pleasant.

Pro 9:18 But he knoweth not that the dead *are* there; *and that* her guests *are* in the depths of hell.

Proverbs 10 through 22:16: "Some Other Proverbs of Solomon"

Proverbs 10

Pro 10:1 The proverbs of Solomon. A wise son maketh a glad father: but a foolish son *is* the heaviness of his mother.

Pro 10:2 Treasures of wickedness profit nothing: but righteousness delivereth from death.

Pro 10:3 The LORD will not suffer the soul of the righteous to famish: but he **(the LORD)** casteth away the substance of the wicked.

Pro 10:4 He becometh poor that dealeth *with* a slack **(or lazy)** hand: but the hand of the diligent maketh rich.

Pro 10:5 He that gathereth in summer *is* a wise son: *but* he that sleepeth in harvest *is* a son that causeth shame.

Pro 10:6 Blessings *are* upon the head of the just: but violence covereth the mouth of the wicked.

Pro 10:7 The memory of the just *is* blessed: but the name of the wicked shall rot.

Pro 10:8 The wise in heart will receive commandments: but a prating *(or foolish talking)* fool shall fall.

Pro 10:9 He that walketh uprightly walketh surely: but he that perverteth his ways shall be known.

Pro 10:10 He that winketh with the eye causeth sorrow: but a prating *(or foolish talking)* fool shall fall.

Pro 10:11 The mouth of a righteous *man is* a well of life: but violence covereth the mouth of the wicked.

Pro 10:12 Hatred stirreth up strifes: but love covereth all sins.

Pro 10:13 In the lips of him that hath understanding wisdom is found: but a rod *(or stick of correction) is* for the back *(side)* of him that is void of understanding.

Pro 10:14 Wise *men* lay up knowledge: but the mouth of the foolish *is* near destruction.

Pro 10:15 The rich man's wealth *is* his strong city: the destruction of the poor *is* their poverty.

Pro 10:16 The labour of the righteous *tendeth* to life: the fruit of the wicked to sin.

Pro 10:17 He *is in* the way of life that keepeth instruction: but he that refuseth reproof *(or correction)* erreth.

Pro 10:18 He that hideth hatred *with* lying lips, and he that uttereth a slander, *is* a fool.

Pro 10:19 In the multitude of words there wanteth not sin: but he that refraineth his lips *is* wise.

Pro 10:20 The tongue of the just *is as* choice silver: the heart of the wicked *is* little worth.

Pro 10:21 The lips of the righteous feed many: but fools die for want of wisdom.

Pro 10:22 The blessing of the LORD, it maketh rich, and he addeth no sorrow with it.

Pro 10:23 *It is* as sport to a fool to do mischief: but a man of understanding hath wisdom.

Pro 10:24 The fear of the wicked, it shall come upon him: but the desire of the righteous shall be granted.

Pro 10:25 As the whirlwind passeth, so *is* the wicked no *more:* but the righteous *is* an everlasting foundation.

Pro 10:26 As vinegar to the teeth, and as smoke to the eyes, so *is* the sluggard to them that send him.

Pro 10:27 The fear of the LORD prolongeth days: but the years of the wicked shall be shortened.

Pro 10:28 The hope of the righteous *shall be* gladness: but the expectation of the wicked shall perish.

Pro 10:29 The way of the LORD *is* strength to the upright: but destruction *shall be* to the workers of iniquity.

Pro 10:30 The righteous shall never be removed: but the wicked shall not inhabit the earth.

Pro 10:31 The mouth of the just bringeth forth wisdom: but the froward *(or contrary)* tongue shall be cut out.

Pro 10:32 The lips of the righteous know what is acceptable: but the mouth of the wicked *speaketh* frowardness.

Proverbs 11

Pro 11:1 A false balance *is* abomination to the LORD: but a just weight *is* his delight **(This concerns merchants that cheat customers by setting their scales (or balances) to indicate false weight readings when they sell their products)**.

Pro 11:2 *When* pride cometh, then cometh shame: but with the lowly *is* wisdom.

Pro 11:3 The integrity of the upright shall guide them: but the perverseness of transgressors shall destroy them.

Pro 11:4 Riches profit not in the day of wrath: but righteousness delivereth from death.

Pro 11:5 The righteousness of the perfect shall direct his way: but the wicked shall fall by his own wickedness.

Pro 11:6 The righteousness of the upright shall deliver them: but transgressors shall be taken in *their own* naughtiness.

Pro 11:7 When a wicked man dieth, *his* expectation shall perish: and the hope of unjust *men* perisheth.

Pro 11:8 The righteous is delivered out of trouble, and the wicked cometh in his stead.

Pro 11:9 An hypocrite with *his* mouth destroyeth his neighbour: but through knowledge shall the just be delivered.

Pro 11:10 When it goeth well with the righteous, the city rejoiceth: and when the wicked perish, *there is* shouting.

Pro 11:11 By the blessing of the upright the city is exalted: but it is overthrown by the mouth of the wicked.

Pro 11:12 He that is void of wisdom despiseth his neighbour: but a man of understanding holdeth his peace.

Pro 11:13 A talebearer revealeth secrets: but he that is of a faithful spirit concealeth the matter.

Pro 11:14 Where no counsel *is*, the people fall: but in the multitude of counsellors *there is* safety.

Pro 11:15 He that is surety **(guarantee; co-sign)** for a stranger shall smart **(or be injured)** *for it:* and he that hateth suretiship **(to make good for another's debt)** is sure **(or secure)**.

Pro 11:16 A gracious woman retaineth honour: and strong *men* retain riches.

Pro 11:17 The merciful man doeth good to his own soul: but *he that is* cruel troubleth his own flesh.

Pro 11:18 The wicked worketh a deceitful work: but to him that soweth righteousness *shall be* a sure reward.

Pro 11:19 As righteousness *tendeth* to life: so he that pursueth evil *pursueth it* to his own death.

Pro 11:20 They that are of a froward heart *are* abomination to the LORD: but *such as are* upright in *their* way *are* his delight.

Pro 11:21 *Though* hand *join* in hand, the wicked shall not be unpunished: but the seed of the righteous shall be delivered.

Pro 11:22 *As* a jewel of gold in a swine's snout, *so is* a fair woman which is without discretion.

Pro 11:23 The desire of the righteous *is* only good: *but* the expectation of the wicked *is* wrath.

Pro 11:24 There is that scattereth, and yet increaseth; and *there is* that withholdeth more than is meet, but *it tendeth* to poverty.

Pro 11:25 The liberal soul shall be made fat: and he that watereth shall be watered also himself.

Pro 11:26 He that withholdeth corn, the people shall curse him: but blessing *shall be* upon the head of him that selleth *it*.

Pro 11:27 He that diligently seeketh good procureth favour: but he that seeketh mischief, it shall come unto him.

Pro 11:28 He that trusteth in his riches shall fall: but the righteous shall flourish as a branch.

Pro 11:29 He that troubleth his own house shall inherit the wind: and the fool *shall be* servant to the wise of heart.

Pro 11:30 The fruit of the righteous *is* a tree of life; and he that winneth souls *is* wise.

Pro 11:31 Behold, the righteous shall be recompensed in the earth: much more the wicked and the sinner.

Proverbs 12

Pro 12:1 Whoso loveth instruction loveth knowledge: but he that hateth reproof *(disapproval) is* brutish.

Pro 12:2 A good *man* obtaineth favour of the LORD: but a man of wicked devices will he condemn.

Pro 12:3 A man shall not be established by wickedness: but the root of the righteous shall not be moved.

Pro 12:4 A virtuous woman *is* a crown to her husband: but she that maketh ashamed *is* as rottenness in his bones.

Pro 12:5 The thoughts of the righteous *are* right: *but* the counsels of the wicked *are* deceit.

Pro 12:6 The words of the wicked *are* to lie in wait for blood: but the mouth of the upright shall deliver them.

Pro 12:7 The wicked are overthrown, and *are* not: but the house of the righteous shall stand.

Pro 12:8 A man shall be commended according to his wisdom: but he that is of a perverse heart shall be despised.

Pro 12:9 *He that is* despised, and hath a servant, *is* better than he that honoureth himself, and lacketh bread.

Pro 12:10 A righteous *man* regardeth the life of his beast: but the tender mercies of the wicked *are* cruel.

Pro 12:11 He that tilleth his land shall be satisfied with bread: but he that followeth vain *persons is* void of understanding.

Pro 12:12 The wicked desireth the net of evil *men:* but the root of the righteous yieldeth *fruit.*

Pro 12:13 The wicked is snared by the transgression of *his* lips: but the just shall come out of trouble.

Pro 12:14 A man shall be satisfied with good by the fruit of *his* mouth: and the recompence of a man's hands shall be rendered unto him.

Pro 12:15 The way of a fool *is* right in his own eyes: but he that hearkeneth unto counsel *is* wise.

Pro 12:16 A fool's wrath is presently known: but a prudent *man* covereth shame.

Pro 12:17 *He that* speaketh truth sheweth forth righteousness: but a false witness deceit.

Pro 12:18 There is that speaketh like the piercings of a sword: but the tongue of the wise *is* health.

Pro 12:19 The lip of truth shall be established for ever: but a lying tongue *is* but for a moment.

Pro 12:20 Deceit *is* in the heart of them that imagine evil: but to the counsellors of peace *is* joy.

Pro 12:21 There shall no evil happen to the just: but the wicked shall be filled with mischief.

Pro 12:22 Lying lips *are* abomination to the LORD: but they that deal truly *are* his delight.

Pro 12:23 A prudent man concealeth knowledge: but the heart of fools proclaimeth foolishness.

Pro 12:24 The hand of the diligent shall bear rule: but the slothful shall be under tribute.

Pro 12:25 Heaviness in the heart of man maketh it stoop: but a good word maketh it glad.

Pro 12:26 The righteous *is* more excellent than his neighbour: but the way of the wicked seduceth them.

Pro 12:27 The slothful *man* roasteth not that which he took in hunting: but the substance of a diligent man *is* precious.

Pro 12:28 In the way of righteousness *is* life; and *in* the pathway *thereof there is* no death.

Proverbs 13

Pro 13:1 A wise son *heareth* his father's instruction: but a scorner heareth not rebuke.

Pro 13:2 A man shall eat good by the fruit of *his* mouth: but the soul of the transgressors *shall eat* violence.

Pro 13:3 He that keepeth his mouth keepeth his life: *but* he that openeth wide his lips shall have destruction.

Pro 13:4 The soul of the sluggard desireth, and *hath* nothing: but the soul of the diligent shall be made fat.

Pro 13:5 A righteous *man* hateth lying: but a wicked *man* is loathsome, and cometh to shame.

Pro 13:6 Righteousness keepeth *him that is* upright in the way: but wickedness overthroweth the sinner.

Pro 13:7 There is that maketh himself rich, yet *hath* nothing: *there is* that maketh himself poor, yet *hath* great riches.

Pro 13:8 The ransom of a man's life *are* his riches: but the poor heareth not rebuke.

Pro 13:9 The light of the righteous rejoiceth: but the lamp of the wicked shall be put out.

Pro 13:10 Only by pride cometh contention: but with the well advised *is* wisdom.

Pro 13:11 Wealth *gotten* by vanity shall be diminished: but he that gathereth by labour shall increase.

Pro 13:12 Hope deferred maketh the heart sick: but *when* the desire cometh, *it is* a tree of life.

Pro 13:13 Whoso despiseth the word shall be destroyed: but he that feareth the commandment shall be rewarded.

Pro 13:14 The law of the wise *is* a fountain of life, to depart from the snares of death.

Pro 13:15 Good understanding giveth favour: but the way of transgressors *is* hard.

Pro 13:16 Every prudent *man* dealeth with knowledge: but a fool layeth open *his* folly.

Pro 13:17 A wicked messenger falleth into mischief: but a faithful ambassador *is* health.

Pro 13:18 Poverty and shame *shall be to* him that refuseth instruction: but he that regardeth reproof shall be honoured.

Pro 13:19 The desire accomplished is sweet to the soul: but *it is* abomination to fools to depart from evil.

Pro 13:20 He that walketh with wise *men* shall be wise: but a companion of fools shall be destroyed.

Pro 13:21 Evil pursueth sinners: but to the righteous good shall be repayed.

Pro 13:22 A good *man* leaveth an inheritance to his children's children: and the wealth of the sinner *is* laid up for the just.

Pro 13:23 Much food *is in* the tillage of the poor: but there is *that is* destroyed for want of judgment.

Pro 13:24 He that spareth his rod hateth his son: but he that loveth him chasteneth him betimes.

Pro 13:25 The righteous eateth to the satisfying of his soul: but the belly of the wicked shall want.

Proverbs 14

Pro 14:1 Every wise woman buildeth her house: but the foolish plucketh it down with her hands *(or her behavior?)*.

Pro 14:2 He that walketh in his uprightness feareth the LORD: but *he that is* perverse in his ways despiseth him.

Pro 14:3 In the mouth of the foolish *is* a rod of pride: but the lips of the wise shall preserve them.

Pro 14:4 Where no oxen *are*, the crib *is* clean: but much increase *is* by the strength of the ox.

Pro 14:5 A faithful witness will not lie: but a false witness will utter lies.

Pro 14:6 A scorner seeketh wisdom, and *findeth it* not: but knowledge *is* easy unto him that understandeth.

Pro 14:7 Go from the presence of a foolish man, when thou perceivest not *in him* the lips of knowledge.

Pro 14:8 The wisdom of the prudent *is* to understand his way: but the folly of fools *is* deceit.

Pro 14:9 Fools make a mock at sin: but among the righteous *there is* favour.

Pro 14:10 The heart knoweth his own bitterness; and a stranger doth not intermeddle with his joy.

Pro 14:11 The house of the wicked shall be overthrown: but the tabernacle of the upright shall flourish.

Pro 14:12 There is a way which seemeth right unto a man, but the end thereof *are* the ways of death.

Pro 14:13 Even in laughter the heart is sorrowful; and the end of that mirth *is* heaviness.

Pro 14:14 The backslider in heart shall be filled with his own ways: and a good man *shall be satisfied* from himself.

Pro 14:15 The simple believeth every word: but the prudent *man* looketh well to his going.

Pro 14:16 A wise *man* feareth, and departeth from evil: but the fool rageth, and is confident.

Pro 14:17 *He that is* soon angry dealeth foolishly: and a man of wicked devices is hated.

Pro 14:18 The simple inherit folly: but the prudent are crowned with knowledge.

Pro 14:19 The evil bow before the good; and the wicked at the gates of the righteous.

Pro 14:20 The poor is hated even of his own neighbour: but the rich *hath* many friends.

Pro 14:21 He that despiseth his neighbour sinneth: but he that hath mercy on the poor, happy *is* he.

Pro 14:22 Do they not err that devise evil? but mercy and truth *shall be* to them that devise good.

Pro 14:23 In all labour there is profit: but the talk of the lips *tendeth* only to penury.

Pro 14:24 The crown of the wise *is* their riches: *but* the foolishness of fools *is* folly.

Pro 14:25 A true witness delivereth souls: but a deceitful *witness* speaketh lies.

Pro 14:26 In the fear of the LORD *is* strong confidence: and his children shall have a place of refuge.

Pro 14:27 The fear of the LORD *is* a fountain of life, to depart from the snares of death.

Pro 14:28 In the multitude of people *is* the king's honour: but in the want of people *is* the destruction of the prince.

Pro 14:29 *He that is* slow to wrath *is* of great understanding: but *he that is* hasty of spirit exalteth folly.

Pro 14:30 A sound heart *is* the life of the flesh: but envy the rottenness of the bones.

Pro 14:31 He that oppresseth the poor reproacheth his Maker: but he that honoureth him hath mercy on the poor.

Pro 14:32 The wicked is driven away in his wickedness: but the righteous hath hope in his death.

Pro 14:33 Wisdom resteth in the heart of him that hath understanding: but *that which is* in the midst of fools is made known.

Pro 14:34 Righteousness exalteth a nation: but sin *is* a reproach to any people.

Pro 14:35 The king's favour *is* toward a wise servant: but his wrath is *against* him that causeth shame.

Proverbs 15

Pro 15:1 A soft answer turneth away wrath: but grievous words stir up anger.

Pro 15:2 The tongue of the wise useth knowledge aright: but the mouth of fools poureth out foolishness.

Pro 15:3 The eyes of the LORD *are* in every place, beholding the evil and the good.

Pro 15:4 A wholesome tongue *is* a tree of life: but perverseness therein *is* a breach in the spirit.

Pro 15:5 A fool despiseth his father's instruction: but he that regardeth reproof is prudent.

Pro 15:6 In the house of the righteous *is* much treasure: but in the revenues of the wicked is trouble.

Pro 15:7 The lips of the wise disperse knowledge: but the heart of the foolish *doeth* not so.

Pro 15:8 The sacrifice of the wicked *is* an abomination to the LORD: but the prayer of the upright *is* his delight.

Pro 15:9 The way of the wicked *is* an abomination unto the LORD: but he loveth him that followeth after righteousness.

Pro 15:10 Correction *is* grievous unto him that forsaketh the way: *and* he that hateth reproof shall die.

Pro 15:11 Hell and destruction *are* before the LORD: how much more then the hearts of the children of men?

Pro 15:12 A scorner loveth not one that reproveth him: neither will he go unto the wise.

Pro 15:13 A merry heart maketh a cheerful countenance: but by sorrow of the heart the spirit is broken.

Pro 15:14 The heart of him that hath understanding seeketh knowledge: but the mouth of fools feedeth on foolishness.

Pro 15:15 All the days of the afflicted *are* evil: but he that is of a merry heart *hath* a continual feast.

Pro 15:16 Better *is* little with the fear of the LORD than great treasure and trouble therewith.

Pro 15:17 Better *is* a dinner of herbs where love is, than a stalled ox and hatred therewith.

Pro 15:18 A wrathful man stirreth up strife: but *he that is* slow to anger appeaseth strife.

Pro 15:19 The way of the slothful *man is* as an hedge of thorns: but the way of the righteous *is* made plain.

Pro 15:20 A wise son maketh a glad father: but a foolish man despiseth his mother.

Pro 15:21 Folly *is* joy to *him that is* destitute of wisdom: but a man of understanding walketh uprightly.

Pro 15:22 Without counsel purposes are disappointed: but in the multitude of counsellors they are established.

Pro 15:23 A man hath joy by the answer of his mouth: and a word *spoken* in due season, how good *is it!*

Pro 15:24 The way of life *is* above to the wise, that he may depart from hell beneath.

Pro 15:25 The LORD will destroy the house of the proud: but he will establish the border of the widow.

Pro 15:26 The thoughts of the wicked *are* an abomination to the LORD: but *the words* of the pure *are* pleasant words.

Pro 15:27 He that is greedy of gain troubleth his own house; but he that hateth gifts shall live.

Pro 15:28 The heart of the righteous studieth to answer: but the mouth of the wicked poureth out evil things.

Pro 15:29 The LORD *is* far from the wicked: but he heareth the prayer of the righteous.

Pro 15:30 The light of the eyes rejoiceth the heart: *and* a good report maketh the bones fat.

Pro 15:31 The ear that heareth the reproof of life abideth among the wise.

Pro 15:32 He that refuseth instruction despiseth his own soul: but he that heareth reproof getteth understanding.

Pro 15:33 The fear of the LORD *is* the instruction of wisdom; and before honour *is* humility.

Proverbs 16

Pro 16:1 The preparations of the heart in man, and the answer of the tongue, *is* from the LORD.

Pro 16:2 All the ways of a man *are* clean in his own eyes; but the LORD weigheth the spirits.

Pro 16:3 Commit thy works unto the LORD, and thy thoughts shall be established.

Pro 16:4 The LORD hath made all *things* for himself: yea, even the wicked for the day of evil.

Pro 16:5 Every one *that is* proud in heart *is* an abomination to the LORD: *though* hand *join* in hand, he shall not be unpunished.

Pro 16:6 By mercy and truth iniquity is purged: and by the fear of the LORD *men* depart from evil.

Pro 16:7 When a man's ways please the LORD, he maketh even his enemies to be at peace with him.

Pro 16:8 Better *is* a little with righteousness than great revenues without right.

Pro 16:9 A man's heart deviseth his way: but the LORD directeth his steps.

Pro 16:10 A divine sentence *is* in the lips of the king: his mouth transgresseth not in judgment.

Pro 16:11 A just weight and balance *are* the LORD'S: all the weights of the bag *are* his work.

Pro 16:12 *It is* an abomination to kings to commit wickedness: for the throne is established by righteousness.

Pro 16:13 Righteous lips *are* the delight of kings; and they love him that speaketh right.

Pro 16:14 The wrath of a king *is as* messengers of death: but a wise man will pacify it.

Pro 16:15 In the light of the king's countenance *is* life; and his favour *is* as a cloud of the latter rain.

Pro 16:16 How much better *is it* to get wisdom than gold! and to get understanding rather to be chosen than silver!

Pro 16:17 The highway of the upright *is* to depart from evil: he that keepeth his way preserveth his soul.

Pro 16:18 Pride *goeth* before destruction, and an haughty spirit before a fall.

Pro 16:19 Better *it is to be* of an humble spirit with the lowly, than to divide the spoil with the proud.

Pro 16:20 He that handleth a matter wisely shall find good: and whoso trusteth in the LORD, happy *is* he.

Pro 16:21 The wise in heart shall be called prudent: and the sweetness of the lips increaseth learning.

Pro 16:22 Understanding *is* a wellspring of life unto him that hath it: but the instruction of fools *is* folly.

Pro 16:23 The heart of the wise teacheth his mouth, and addeth learning to his lips.

Pro 16:24 Pleasant words *are as* an honeycomb, sweet to the soul, and health to the bones.

Pro 16:25 There is a way that seemeth right unto a man, but the end thereof *are* the ways of death.

Pro 16:26 He that laboureth laboureth for himself; for his mouth craveth it of him.

Pro 16:27 An ungodly man diggeth up evil: and in his lips *there is* as a burning fire.

Pro 16:28 A froward man soweth strife: and a whisperer separateth chief friends.

Pro 16:29 A violent man enticeth his neighbour, and leadeth him into the way *that is* not good.

Pro 16:30 He shutteth his eyes to devise froward things: moving his lips he bringeth evil to pass.

Pro 16:31 The hoary head *is* a crown of glory, *if* it be found in the way of righteousness.

Pro 16:32 *He that is* slow to anger *is* better than the mighty; and he that ruleth his spirit than he that taketh a city.

Pro 16:33 The lot is cast into the lap; but the whole disposing thereof *is* of the LORD.

Proverbs 17

Pro 17:1 Better *is* a dry morsel, and quietness therewith, than an house full of sacrifices *with* strife.

Pro 17:2 A wise servant shall have rule over a son that causeth shame, and shall have part of the inheritance among the brethren.

Pro 17:3 The fining pot *is* for silver, and the furnace for gold: but the LORD trieth the hearts.

Pro 17:4 A wicked doer giveth heed to false lips; *and* a liar giveth ear to a naughty tongue.

Pro 17:5 Whoso mocketh the poor reproacheth his Maker: *and* he that is glad at calamities shall not be unpunished.

Pro 17:6 Children's children *are* the crown of old men; and the glory of children *are* their fathers.

Pro 17:7 Excellent speech becometh not a fool: much less do lying lips a prince.

Pro 17:8 A gift *is as* a precious stone in the eyes of him that hath it: whithersoever it turneth, it prospereth.

Pro 17:9 He that covereth a transgression seeketh love; but he that repeateth a matter separateth *very* friends.

Pro 17:10 A reproof entereth more into a wise man than an hundred stripes into a fool.

Pro 17:11 An evil *man* seeketh only rebellion: therefore a cruel messenger shall be sent against him.

Pro 17:12 Let a bear robbed of her whelps meet a man, rather than a fool in his folly.

Pro 17:13 Whoso rewardeth evil for good, evil shall not depart from his house.

Pro 17:14 The beginning of strife *is as* when one letteth out water: therefore leave off contention, before it be meddled with.

Pro 17:15 He that justifieth the wicked, and he that condemneth the just, even they both *are* abomination to the LORD.

Pro 17:16 Wherefore *is there* a price in the hand of a fool to get wisdom, seeing *he hath* no heart *to it?*

Pro 17:17 A friend loveth at all times, and a brother is born for adversity.

Pro 17:18 A man void of understanding striketh hands, *and* becometh surety in the presence of his friend.

Pro 17:19 He loveth transgression that loveth strife: *and* he that exalteth his gate seeketh destruction.

Pro 17:20 He that hath a froward heart findeth no good: and he that hath a perverse tongue falleth into mischief.

Pro 17:21 He that begetteth a fool *doeth it* to his sorrow: and the father of a fool hath no joy.

Pro 17:22 A merry heart doeth good *like* a medicine: but a broken spirit drieth the bones.

Pro 17:23 A wicked *man* taketh a gift out of the bosom to pervert the ways of judgment.

Pro 17:24 Wisdom *is* before him that hath understanding; but the eyes of a fool *are* in the ends of the earth.

Pro 17:25 A foolish son *is* a grief to his father, and bitterness to her that bare him.

Pro 17:26 Also to punish the just *is* not good, *nor* to strike princes for equity.

Pro 17:27 He that hath knowledge spareth his words: *and* a man of understanding is of an excellent spirit.

Pro 17:28 Even a fool, when he holdeth his peace, is counted wise: *and* he that shutteth his lips *is esteemed* a man of understanding.

Proverbs 18

Pro 18:1 Through desire a man, having separated himself, seeketh *and* intermeddleth with all wisdom.

Pro 18:2 A fool hath no delight in understanding, but that his heart may discover itself.

Pro 18:3 When the wicked cometh, *then* cometh also contempt, and with ignominy reproach.

Pro 18:4 The words of a man's mouth *are as* deep waters, *and* the wellspring of wisdom *as* a flowing brook.

Pro 18:5 *It is* not good to accept the person of the wicked, to overthrow the righteous in judgment.

Pro 18:6 A fool's lips enter into contention, and his mouth calleth for strokes.

Pro 18:7 A fool's mouth *is* his destruction, and his lips *are* the snare of his soul.

Pro 18:8 The words of a talebearer *are* as wounds, and they go down into the innermost parts of the belly.

Pro 18:9 He also that is slothful in his work is brother to him that is a great waster.

Pro 18:10 The name of the LORD *is* a strong tower: the righteous runneth into it, and is safe.

Pro 18:11 The rich man's wealth *is* his strong city, and as an high wall in his own conceit.

Pro 18:12 Before destruction the heart of man is haughty, and before honour *is* humility.

Pro 18:13 He that answereth a matter before he heareth *it*, it *is* folly and shame unto him.

Pro 18:14 The spirit of a man will sustain his infirmity; but a wounded spirit who can bear?

Pro 18:15 The heart of the prudent getteth knowledge; and the ear of the wise seeketh knowledge.

Pro 18:16 A man's gift maketh room for him, and bringeth him before great men.

Pro 18:17 *He that is* first in his own cause *seemeth* just; but his neighbour cometh and searcheth him.

Pro 18:18 The lot causeth contentions to cease, and parteth between the mighty.

Pro 18:19 A brother offended *is harder to be won* than a strong city: and *their* contentions *are* like the bars of a castle.

Pro 18:20 A man's belly shall be satisfied with the fruit of his mouth; *and* with the increase of his lips shall he be filled.

Pro 18:21 Death and life *are* in the power of the tongue: and they that love it shall eat the fruit thereof.

Pro 18:22 *Whoso* findeth a wife findeth a good *thing*, and obtaineth favour of the LORD.

Pro 18:23 The poor useth intreaties; but the rich answereth roughly.

Pro 18:24 A man *that hath* friends must shew himself friendly: and there is a friend *that* sticketh closer than a brother.

Proverbs 19

Pro 19:1 Better *is* the poor that walketh in his integrity, than *he that is* perverse in his lips, and is a fool.

Pro 19:2 Also, *that* the soul *be* without knowledge, *it is* not good; and he that hasteth with *his* feet sinneth.

Pro 19:3 The foolishness of man perverteth his way: and his heart fretteth against the LORD.

Pro 19:4 Wealth maketh many friends; but the poor is separated from his neighbour.

Pro 19:5 A false witness shall not be unpunished, and *he that* speaketh lies shall not escape.

Pro 19:6 Many will intreat the favour of the prince: and every man *is* a friend to him that giveth gifts.

Pro 19:7 All the brethren of the poor do hate him: how much more do his friends go far from him? he pursueth *them with* words, *yet* they *are* wanting *to him*.

Pro 19:8 He that getteth wisdom loveth his own soul: he that keepeth understanding shall find good.

Pro 19:9 A false witness shall not be unpunished, and *he that* speaketh lies shall perish.

Pro 19:10 Delight is not seemly for a fool; much less for a servant to have rule over princes.

Pro 19:11 The discretion of a man deferreth his anger; and *it is* his glory to pass over a transgression.

Pro 19:12 The king's wrath *is* as the roaring of a lion; but his favour *is* as dew upon the grass.

Pro 19:13 A foolish son *is* the calamity of his father: and the contentions of a wife *are* a continual dropping.

Pro 19:14 House and riches *are* the inheritance of fathers: and a prudent wife *is* from the LORD.

Pro 19:15 Slothfulness casteth into a deep sleep; and an idle soul shall suffer hunger.

Pro 19:16 He that keepeth the commandment keepeth his own soul; *but* he that despiseth his ways shall die.

Pro 19:17 He that hath pity upon the poor lendeth unto the LORD; and that which he hath given will he pay him again.

Pro 19:18 Chasten thy son while there is hope, and let not thy soul spare for his crying.

Pro 19:19 A man of great wrath shall suffer punishment: for if thou deliver *him*, yet thou must do it again.

Pro 19:20 Hear counsel, and receive instruction, that thou mayest be wise in thy latter end.

Pro 19:21 *There are* many devices in a man's heart; nevertheless the counsel of the LORD, that shall stand.

Pro 19:22 The desire of a man *is* his kindness: and a poor man *is* better than a liar.

Pro 19:23 The fear of the LORD *tendeth* to life: and *he that hath it* shall abide satisfied; he shall not be visited with evil.

Pro 19:24 A slothful *man* hideth his hand in *his* bosom, and will not so much as bring it to his mouth again.

Pro 19:25 Smite a scorner, and the simple will beware: and reprove one that hath understanding, *and* he will understand knowledge.

Pro 19:26 He that wasteth *his* father, *and* chaseth away *his* mother, *is* a son that causeth shame, and bringeth reproach.

Pro 19:27 Cease, my son, to hear the instruction *that causeth* to err from the words of knowledge.

Pro 19:28 An ungodly witness scorneth judgment: and the mouth of the wicked devoureth iniquity.

Pro 19:29 Judgments are prepared for scorners, and stripes for the back of fools.

Proverbs 20

Pro 20:1 Wine *is* a mocker, strong drink *is* raging: and whosoever is deceived thereby is not wise.

Pro 20:2 The fear of a king *is* as the roaring of a lion: *whoso* provoketh him to anger sinneth *against* his own soul.

Pro 20:3 *It is* an honour for a man to cease from strife: but every fool will be meddling.

Pro 20:4 The sluggard will not plow by reason of the cold; *therefore* shall he beg in harvest, and *have* nothing.

Pro 20:5 Counsel in the heart of man *is like* deep water; but a man of understanding will draw it out.

Pro 20:6 Most men will proclaim every one his own goodness: but a faithful man who can find?

Pro 20:7 The just *man* walketh in his integrity: his children *are* blessed after him.

Pro 20:8 A king that sitteth in the throne of judgment scattereth away all evil with his eyes.

Pro 20:9 Who can say, I have made my heart clean, I am pure from my sin?

Pro 20:10 Divers weights, *and* divers measures, both of them *are* alike abomination to the LORD.

Pro 20:11 Even a child is known by his doings, whether his work *be* pure, and whether *it be* right.

Pro 20:12 The hearing ear, and the seeing eye, the LORD hath made even both of them.

Pro 20:13 Love not sleep, lest thou come to poverty; open thine eyes, *and* thou shalt be satisfied with bread.

Pro 20:14 *It is* naught, *it is* naught, saith the buyer: but when he is gone his way, then he boasteth.

Pro 20:15 There is gold, and a multitude of rubies: but the lips of knowledge *are* a precious jewel.

Pro 20:16 Take his garment that is surety *for* a stranger: and take a pledge of him for a strange woman.

Pro 20:17 Bread of deceit *is* sweet to a man; but afterwards his mouth shall be filled with gravel.

Pro 20:18 *Every* purpose is established by counsel: and with good advice make war.

Pro 20:19 He that goeth about *as* a talebearer revealeth secrets: therefore meddle not with him that flattereth with his lips.

Pro 20:20 Whoso curseth his father or his mother, his lamp shall be put out in obscure darkness.

Pro 20:21 An inheritance *may be* gotten hastily at the beginning; but the end thereof shall not be blessed.

Pro 20:22 Say not thou, I will recompense evil; *but* wait on the LORD, and he shall save thee.

Pro 20:23 Divers weights *are* an abomination unto the LORD; and a false balance *is* not good.

Pro 20:24 Man's goings *are* of the LORD; how can a man then understand his own way?

Pro 20:25 *It is* a snare to the man *who* devoureth *that which is* holy, and after vows to make enquiry.

Pro 20:26 A wise king scattereth the wicked, and bringeth the wheel over them.

Pro 20:27 The spirit of man *is* the candle of the LORD, searching all the inward parts of the belly.

Pro 20:28 Mercy and truth preserve the king: and his throne is upholden by mercy.

Pro 20:29 The glory of young men *is* their strength: and the beauty of old men *is* the gray head.

Pro 20:30 The blueness of a wound cleanseth away evil: so *do* stripes the inward parts of the belly.

Proverbs 21

Pro 21:1 The king's heart *is* in the hand of the LORD, *as* the rivers of water: he turneth it whithersoever he will.

Pro 21:2 Every way of a man *is* right in his own eyes: but the LORD pondereth the hearts.

Pro 21:3 To do justice and judgment *is* more acceptable to the LORD than sacrifice.

Pro 21:4 An high look, and a proud heart, *and* the plowing of the wicked, *is* sin.

Pro 21:5 The thoughts of the diligent *tend* only to plenteousness; but of every one *that is* hasty only to want.

Pro 21:6 The getting of treasures by a lying tongue *is* a vanity tossed to and fro of them that seek death.

Pro 21:7 The robbery of the wicked shall destroy them; because they refuse to do judgment.

Pro 21:8 The way of man *is* froward and strange: but *as for* the pure, his work *is* right.

Pro 21:9 *It is* better to dwell in a corner of the housetop, than with a brawling woman in a wide house.

Pro 21:10 The soul of the wicked desireth evil: his neighbour findeth no favour in his eyes.

Pro 21:11 When the scorner is punished, the simple is made wise: and when the wise is instructed, he receiveth knowledge.

Pro 21:12 The righteous *man* wisely considereth the house of the wicked: *but God* overthroweth the wicked for *their* wickedness.

Pro 21:13 Whoso stoppeth his ears at the cry of the poor, he also shall cry himself, but shall not be heard.

Pro 21:14 A gift in secret pacifieth anger: and a reward in the bosom strong wrath.

Pro 21:15 *It is* joy to the just to do judgment: but destruction *shall be* to the workers of iniquity.

Pro 21:16 The man that wandereth out of the way of understanding shall remain in the congregation of the dead.

Pro 21:17 He that loveth pleasure *shall be* a poor man: he that loveth wine and oil shall not be rich.

Pro 21:18 The wicked *shall be* a ransom for the righteous, and the transgressor for the upright.

Pro 21:19 *It is* better to dwell in the wilderness, than with a contentious and an angry woman.

Pro 21:20 *There is* treasure to be desired and oil in the dwelling of the wise; but a foolish man spendeth it up.

Pro 21:21 He that followeth after righteousness and mercy findeth life, righteousness, and honour.

Pro 21:22 A wise *man* scaleth the city of the mighty, and casteth down the strength of the confidence thereof.

Pro 21:23 Whoso keepeth his mouth and his tongue keepeth his soul from troubles.

Pro 21:24 Proud *and* haughty scorner *is* his name, who dealeth in proud wrath.

Pro 21:25 The desire of the slothful killeth him; for his hands refuse to labour.

Pro 21:26 He coveteth greedily all the day long: but the righteous giveth and spareth not.

Pro 21:27 The sacrifice of the wicked *is* abomination: how much more, *when* he bringeth it with a wicked mind?

Pro 21:28 A false witness shall perish: but the man that heareth speaketh constantly.

Pro 21:29 A wicked man hardeneth his face: but *as for* the upright, he directeth his way.

Pro 21:30 *There is* no wisdom nor understanding nor counsel against the LORD.

Pro 21:31 The horse *is* prepared against the day of battle: but safety *is* of the LORD.

Proverbs 22

Proverbs 22 through 22:16

Pro 22:1 A *good* name *is* rather to be chosen than great riches, *and* loving favour rather than silver and gold.

Pro 22:2 The rich and poor meet together: the LORD *is* the maker of them all.

Pro 22:3 A prudent *man* foreseeth the evil, and hideth himself: but the simple pass on, and are punished.

Pro 22:4 By humility *and* the fear of the LORD *are* riches, and honour, and life.

Pro 22:5 Thorns *and* snares *are* in the way of the froward: he that doth keep his soul shall be far from them.

Pro 22:6 Train up a child in the way he should go: and when he is old, he will not depart from it.

Pro 22:7 The rich ruleth over the poor, and the borrower *is* servant to the lender.

Pro 22:8 He that soweth iniquity shall reap vanity: and the rod of his anger shall fail.

Pro 22:9 He that hath a bountiful eye shall be blessed; for he giveth of his bread to the poor.

Pro 22:10 Cast out the scorner, and contention shall go out; yea, strife and reproach shall cease.

Pro 22:11 He that loveth pureness of heart, *for* the grace of his lips the king *shall be* his friend.

Pro 22:12 The eyes of the LORD preserve knowledge, and he overthroweth the words of the transgressor.

Pro 22:13 The slothful *man* saith, *There is* a lion without, I shall be slain in the streets.

Pro 22:14 The mouth of strange women *is* a deep pit: he that is abhorred of the LORD shall fall therein.

Pro 22:15 Foolishness *is* bound in the heart of a child; *but* the rod of correction shall drive it far from him.

Pro 22:16 He that oppresseth the poor to increase his *riches, and* he that giveth to the rich, *shall* surely *come* to want.

Proverbs 22:17 through 24:34: "The Sayings of the Wise"

More Wise Sayings

Pro 22:17 Bow down thine ear, and hear the words of the wise, and apply thine heart unto my knowledge.

Pro 22:18 For *it is* a pleasant thing if thou keep them within thee; they shall withal be fitted in thy lips.

Pro 22:19 That thy trust may be in the LORD, I have made known to thee this day, even to thee.

Pro 22:20 Have not I written to thee excellent things in counsels and knowledge,

Pro 22:21 That I might make thee know the certainty of the words of truth; that thou mightest answer the words of truth to them that send unto thee?

Pro 22:22 Rob not the poor, because he *is* poor: neither oppress the afflicted in the gate:

Pro 22:23 For the LORD will plead their cause, and spoil the soul of those that spoiled them.

Pro 22:24 Make no friendship with an angry man; and with a furious man thou shalt not go:

Pro 22:25 Lest thou learn his ways, and get a snare to thy soul.

Pro 22:26 Be not thou *one* of them that strike hands, *or* of them that are sureties for debts.

Pro 22:27 If thou hast nothing to pay, why should he take away thy bed from under thee?

Pro 22:28 Remove not the ancient landmark, which thy fathers have set.

Pro 22:29 Seest thou a man diligent in his business? he shall stand before kings; he shall not stand before mean *men*.

Proverbs 23

Pro 23:1 When thou sittest to eat with a ruler, consider diligently what *is* before thee:

Pro 23:2 And put a knife to thy throat, if thou *be* a man given to appetite.

Pro 23:3 Be not desirous of his dainties: for they *are* deceitful meat.

Pro 23:4 Labour not to be rich: cease from thine own wisdom.

Pro 23:5 Wilt thou set thine eyes upon that which is not? for *riches* certainly make themselves wings; they fly away as an eagle toward heaven.

Pro 23:6 Eat thou not the bread of *him that hath* an evil eye, neither desire thou his dainty meats:

Pro 23:7 For as he thinketh in his heart, so *is* he: Eat and drink, saith he to thee; but his heart *is* not with thee.

Pro 23:8 The morsel *which* thou hast eaten shalt thou vomit up, and lose thy sweet words.

Pro 23:9 Speak not in the ears of a fool: for he will despise the wisdom of thy words.

Pro 23:10 Remove not the old landmark; and enter not into the fields of the fatherless:

Pro 23:11 For their redeemer *is* mighty; he shall plead their cause with thee.

Pro 23:12 Apply thine heart unto instruction, and thine ears to the words of knowledge.

Pro 23:13 Withhold not correction from the child: for *if* thou beatest him with the rod, he shall not die.

Pro 23:14 Thou shalt beat him with the rod, and shalt deliver his soul from hell.

Pro 23:15 My son, if thine heart be wise, my heart shall rejoice, even mine.

Pro 23:16 Yea, my reins shall rejoice, when thy lips speak right things.

Pro 23:17 Let not thine heart envy sinners: but *be thou* in the fear of the LORD all the day long.

Pro 23:18 For surely there is an end; and thine expectation shall not be cut off.

Pro 23:19 Hear thou, my son, and be wise, and guide thine heart in the way.

Pro 23:20 Be not among winebibbers; among riotous eaters of flesh:

Pro 23:21 For the drunkard and the glutton shall come to poverty: and drowsiness shall clothe *a man* with rags.

Pro 23:22 Hearken unto thy father that begat thee, and despise not thy mother when she is old.

Pro 23:23 Buy the truth, and sell *it* not; *also* wisdom, and instruction, and understanding.

Pro 23:24 The father of the righteous shall greatly rejoice: and he that begetteth a wise *child* shall have joy of him.

Pro 23:25 Thy father and thy mother shall be glad, and she that bare thee shall rejoice.

Pro 23:26 My son, give me thine heart, and let thine eyes observe my ways.

Pro 23:27 For a whore *is* a deep ditch; and a strange woman *is* a narrow pit.

Pro 23:28 She also lieth in wait as *for* a prey, and increaseth the transgressors among men.

Pro 23:29 Who hath woe? who hath sorrow? who hath contentions? who hath babbling? who hath wounds without cause? who hath redness of eyes?

Pro 23:30 They that tarry long at the wine; they that go to seek mixed wine.

Pro 23:31 Look not thou upon the wine when it is red, when it giveth his colour in the cup, *when* it moveth itself aright.

Pro 23:32 At the last it biteth like a serpent, and stingeth like an adder.

Pro 23:33 Thine eyes shall behold strange women, and thine heart shall utter perverse things.

Pro 23:34 Yea, thou shalt be as he that lieth down in the midst of the sea, or as he that lieth upon the top of a mast.

Pro 23:35 They have stricken me, *shalt thou say, and* I was not sick; they have beaten me, *and* I felt *it* not: when shall I awake? I will seek it yet again.

Proverbs 24

Proverbs 24:1 through 24:22

Pro 24:1 Be not thou envious against evil men, neither desire to be with them.

Pro 24:2 For their heart studieth destruction, and their lips talk of mischief.

Pro 24:3 Through wisdom is an house builded; and by understanding it is established:

Pro 24:4 And by knowledge shall the chambers be filled with all precious and pleasant riches.

Pro 24:5 A wise man *is* strong; yea, a man of knowledge increaseth strength.

Pro 24:6 For by wise counsel thou shalt make thy war: and in multitude of counsellors *there is* safety.

Pro 24:7 Wisdom *is* too high for a fool: he openeth not his mouth in the gate.

Pro 24:8 He that deviseth to do evil shall be called a mischievous person.

Pro 24:9 The thought of foolishness *is* sin: and the scorner *is* an abomination to men.

Pro 24:10 *If* thou faint in the day of adversity, thy strength *is* small.

Pro 24:11 If thou forbear to deliver *them that are* drawn unto death, and *those that are* ready to be slain;

Pro 24:12 If thou sayest, Behold, we knew it not; doth not he that pondereth the heart consider *it?* and he that keepeth thy soul, doth *not* he know *it?* and shall *not* he render to *every* man according to his works?

Pro 24:13 My son, eat thou honey, because *it is* good; and the honeycomb, *which is* sweet to thy taste:

Pro 24:14 So *shall* the knowledge of wisdom *be* unto thy soul: when thou hast found *it*, then there shall be a reward, and thy expectation shall not be cut off.

Pro 24:15 Lay not wait, O wicked *man*, against the dwelling of the righteous; spoil not his resting place:

Pro 24:16 For a just *man* falleth seven times, and riseth up again: but the wicked shall fall into mischief.

Pro 24:17 Rejoice not when thine enemy falleth, and let not thine heart be glad when he stumbleth:

Pro 24:18 Lest the LORD see *it*, and it displease him, and he turn away his wrath from him.

Pro 24:19 Fret not thyself because of evil *men*, neither be thou envious at the wicked;

Pro 24:20 For there shall be no reward to the evil *man;* the candle of the wicked shall be put out.

Pro 24:21 My son, fear thou the LORD and the king: *and* meddle not with them that are given to change:

Pro 24:22 For their calamity shall rise suddenly; and who knoweth the ruin of them both?

Proverbs 24:23 through 24:34

Pro 24:23 These *things* also *belong* to the wise. *It is* not good to have respect of persons in judgment.

Pro 24:24 He that saith unto the wicked, Thou *art* righteous; him shall the people curse, nations shall abhor him:

Pro 24:25 But to them that rebuke *him* shall be delight, and a good blessing shall come upon them.

Pro 24:26 *Every man* shall kiss *his* lips that giveth a right answer.

Pro 24:27 Prepare thy work without, and make it fit for thyself in the field; and afterwards build thine house.

Pro 24:28 Be not a witness against thy neighbour without cause; and deceive *not* with thy lips.

Pro 24:29 Say not, I will do so to him as he hath done to me: I will render to the man according to his work.

Pro 24:30 I went by the field of the slothful, and by the vineyard of the man void of understanding;

Pro 24:31 And, lo, it was all grown over with thorns, *and* nettles had covered the face thereof, and the stone wall thereof was broken down.

Pro 24:32 Then I saw, *and* considered *it* well: I looked upon *it, and* received instruction.

Pro 24:33 *Yet* a little sleep, a little slumber, a little folding of the hands to sleep:

Pro 24:34 So shall thy poverty come *as* one that travelleth; and thy want as an armed man.

Proverbs 25 through 29:27: "More Proverbs of Solomon that the Councilors of King Hezekiah of Judah Compiled"

Proverbs 25

Pro 25:1 These *are* also proverbs of Solomon, which the men of Hezekiah king of Judah copied out.

Pro 25:2 *It is* the glory of God to conceal a thing: but the honour of kings *is* to search out a matter.

Pro 25:3 The heaven for height, and the earth for depth, and the heart of kings *is* unsearchable.

Pro 25:4 Take away the dross from the silver, and there shall come forth a vessel for the finer.

Pro 25:5 Take away the wicked *from* before the king, and his throne shall be established in righteousness.

Pro 25:6 Put not forth thyself in the presence of the king, and stand not in the place of great *men:*

Pro 25:7 For better *it is* that it be said unto thee, Come up hither; than that thou shouldest be put lower in the presence of the prince whom thine eyes have seen.

Pro 25:8 Go not forth hastily to strive, lest *thou know not* what to do in the end thereof, when thy neighbour hath put thee to shame.

Pro 25:9 Debate thy cause with thy neighbour *himself;* and discover not a secret to another:

Pro 25:10 Lest he that heareth *it* put thee to shame, and thine infamy turn not away.

Pro 25:11 A word fitly spoken *is like* apples of gold in pictures of silver.

Pro 25:12 *As* an earring of gold, and an ornament of fine gold, *so is* a wise reprover upon an obedient ear.

Pro 25:13 As the cold of snow in the time of harvest, *so is* a faithful messenger to them that send him: for he refresheth the soul of his masters.

Pro 25:14 Whoso boasteth himself of a false gift *is like* clouds and wind without rain.

Pro 25:15 By long forbearing is a prince persuaded, and a soft tongue breaketh the bone.

Pro 25:16 Hast thou found honey? eat so much as is sufficient for thee, lest thou be filled therewith, and vomit it.

Pro 25:17 Withdraw thy foot from thy neighbour's house; lest he be weary of thee, and *so* hate thee.

Pro 25:18 A man that beareth false witness against his neighbour *is* a maul, and a sword, and a sharp arrow.

Pro 25:19 Confidence in an unfaithful man in time of trouble *is like* a broken tooth, and a foot out of joint.

Pro 25:20 *As* he that taketh away a garment in cold weather, *and as* vinegar upon nitre, so *is* he that singeth songs to an heavy heart.

Pro 25:21 If thine enemy be hungry, give him bread to eat; and if he be thirsty, give him water to drink:

Pro 25:22 For thou shalt heap coals of fire upon his head, and the LORD shall reward thee.

Pro 25:23 The north wind driveth away rain: so *doth* an angry countenance a backbiting tongue.

Pro 25:24 *It is* better to dwell in the corner of the housetop, than with a brawling woman and in a wide house.

Pro 25:25 *As* cold waters to a thirsty soul, so *is* good news from a far country.

Pro 25:26 A righteous man falling down before the wicked *is as* a troubled fountain, and a corrupt spring.

Pro 25:27 *It is* not good to eat much honey: so *for men* to search their own glory *is not* glory.

Pro 25:28 He that *hath* no rule over his own spirit *is like* a city *that is* broken down, *and* without walls.

Proverbs 26

Pro 26:1 As snow in summer, and as rain in harvest, so honour is not seemly for a fool.

Pro 26:2 As the bird by wandering, as the swallow by flying, so the curse causeless shall not come.

Pro 26:3 A whip for the horse, a bridle for the ass, and a rod for the fool's back.

Pro 26:4 Answer not a fool according to his folly, lest thou also be like unto him.

Pro 26:5 Answer a fool according to his folly, lest he be wise in his own conceit.

Pro 26:6 He that sendeth a message by the hand of a fool cutteth off the feet, *and* drinketh damage.

Pro 26:7 The legs of the lame are not equal: so *is* a parable in the mouth of fools.

Pro 26:8 As he that bindeth a stone in a sling, so *is* he that giveth honour to a fool.

Pro 26:9 *As* a thorn goeth up into the hand of a drunkard, so *is* a parable in the mouth of fools.

Pro 26:10 The great *God* that formed all *things* both rewardeth the fool, and rewardeth transgressors.

Pro 26:11 As a dog returneth to his vomit, *so* a fool returneth to his folly.

Pro 26:12 Seest thou a man wise in his own conceit? *there is* more hope of a fool than of him.

Pro 26:13 The slothful *man* saith, *There is* a lion in the way; a lion *is* in the streets.

Pro 26:14 *As* the door turneth upon his hinges, so *doth* the slothful upon his bed.

Pro 26:15 The slothful hideth his hand in *his* bosom; it grieveth him to bring it again to his mouth.

Pro 26:16 The sluggard *is* wiser in his own conceit than seven men that can render a reason.

Pro 26:17 He that passeth by, *and* meddleth with strife *belonging* not to him, *is like* one that taketh a dog by the ears.

Pro 26:18 As a mad *man* who casteth firebrands, arrows, and death,

Pro 26:19 So *is* the man *that* deceiveth his neighbour, and saith, Am not I in sport?

Pro 26:20 Where no wood is, *there* the fire goeth out: so where *there is* no talebearer, the strife ceaseth.

Pro 26:21 *As* coals *are* to burning coals, and wood to fire; so *is* a contentious man to kindle strife.

Pro 26:22 The words of a talebearer *are* as wounds, and they go down into the innermost parts of the belly.

Pro 26:23 Burning lips and a wicked heart *are like* a potsherd covered with silver dross.

Pro 26:24 He that hateth dissembleth with his lips, and layeth up deceit within him;

Pro 26:25 When he speaketh fair, believe him not: for *there are* seven abominations in his heart.

Pro 26:26 *Whose* hatred is covered by deceit, his wickedness shall be shewed before the *whole* congregation.

Pro 26:27 Whoso diggeth a pit shall fall therein: and he that rolleth a stone, it will return upon him.

Pro 26:28 A lying tongue hateth *those that are* afflicted by it; and a flattering mouth worketh ruin.

Proverbs 27

Pro 27:1 Boast not thyself of to morrow; for thou knowest not what a day may bring forth.

Pro 27:2 Let another man praise thee, and not thine own mouth; a stranger, and not thine own lips.

Pro 27:3 A stone *is* heavy, and the sand weighty; but a fool's wrath *is* heavier than them both.

Pro 27:4 Wrath *is* cruel, and anger *is* outrageous; but who *is* able to stand before envy?

Pro 27:5 Open rebuke *is* better than secret love.

Pro 27:6 Faithful *are* the wounds of a friend; but the kisses of an enemy *are* deceitful.

Pro 27:7 The full soul loatheth an honeycomb; but to the hungry soul every bitter thing is sweet.

Pro 27:8 As a bird that wandereth from her nest, so *is* a man that wandereth from his place.

Pro 27:9 Ointment and perfume rejoice the heart: so *doth* the sweetness of a man's friend by hearty counsel.

Pro 27:10 Thine own friend, and thy father's friend, forsake not; neither go into thy brother's house in the day of thy calamity: *for* better *is* a neighbour *that is* near than a brother far off.

Pro 27:11 My son, be wise, and make my heart glad, that I may answer him that reproacheth me.

Pro 27:12 A prudent *man* foreseeth the evil, *and* hideth himself; *but* the simple pass on, *and* are punished.

Pro 27:13 Take his garment that is surety for a stranger, and take a pledge of him for a strange woman.

Pro 27:14 He that blesseth his friend with a loud voice, rising early in the morning, it shall be counted a curse to him.

Pro 27:15 A continual dropping in a very rainy day and a contentious woman are alike.

Pro 27:16 Whosoever hideth her hideth the wind, and the ointment of his right hand, *which* bewrayeth *itself.*

Pro 27:17 Iron sharpeneth iron; so a man sharpeneth the countenance of his friend.

Pro 27:18 Whoso keepeth the fig tree shall eat the fruit thereof: so he that waiteth on his master shall be honoured.

Pro 27:19 As in water face *answereth* to face, so the heart of man to man.

Pro 27:20 Hell and destruction are never full; so the eyes of man are never satisfied.

Pro 27:21 *As* the fining pot for silver, and the furnace for gold; so *is* a man to his praise.

Pro 27:22 Though thou shouldest bray a fool in a mortar among wheat with a pestle, *yet* will not his foolishness depart from him.

Pro 27:23 Be thou diligent to know the state of thy flocks, *and* look well to thy herds.

Pro 27:24 For riches *are* not for ever: and doth the crown *endure* to every generation?

Pro 27:25 The hay appeareth, and the tender grass sheweth itself, and herbs of the mountains are gathered.

Pro 27:26 The lambs *are* for thy clothing, and the goats *are* the price of the field.

Pro 27:27 And *thou shalt have* goats' milk enough for thy food, for the food of thy household, and *for* the maintenance for thy maidens.

Proverbs 28

Pro 28:1 The wicked flee when no man pursueth: but the righteous are bold as a lion.

Pro 28:2 For the transgression of a land many *are* the princes thereof: but by a man of understanding *and* knowledge the state *thereof* shall be prolonged.

Pro 28:3 A poor man that oppresseth the poor *is like* a sweeping rain which leaveth no food.

Pro 28:4 They that forsake the law praise the wicked: but such as keep the law contend with them.

Pro 28:5 Evil men understand not judgment: but they that seek the LORD understand all *things*.

Pro 28:6 Better *is* the poor that walketh in his uprightness, than *he that is* perverse *in his* ways, though he *be* rich.

Pro 28:7 Whoso keepeth the law *is* a wise son: but he that is a companion of riotous *men* shameth his father.

Pro 28:8 He that by usury and unjust gain increaseth his substance, he shall gather it for him that will pity the poor.

Pro 28:9 He that turneth away his ear from hearing the law, even his prayer *shall be* abomination.

Pro 28:10 Whoso causeth the righteous to go astray in an evil way, he shall fall himself into his own pit: but the upright shall have good *things* in possession.

Pro 28:11 The rich man *is* wise in his own conceit; but the poor that hath understanding searcheth him out.

Pro 28:12 When righteous *men* do rejoice, *there is* great glory: but when the wicked rise, a man is hidden.

Pro 28:13 He that covereth his sins shall not prosper: but whoso confesseth and forsaketh *them* shall have mercy.

Pro 28:14 Happy *is* the man that feareth alway: but he that hardeneth his heart shall fall into mischief.

Pro 28:15 *As* a roaring lion, and a ranging bear; *so is* a wicked ruler over the poor people.

Pro 28:16 The prince that wanteth understanding *is* also a great oppressor: *but* he that hateth covetousness shall prolong *his* days.

Pro 28:17 A man that doeth violence to the blood of *any* person shall flee to the pit; let no man stay him.

Pro 28:18 Whoso walketh uprightly shall be saved: but *he that is* perverse *in his* ways shall fall at once.

Pro 28:19 He that tilleth his land shall have plenty of bread: but he that followeth after vain *persons* shall have poverty enough.

Pro 28:20 A faithful man shall abound with blessings: but he that maketh haste to be rich shall not be innocent.

Pro 28:21 To have respect of persons *is* not good: for for a piece of bread *that* man will transgress.

Pro 28:22 He that hasteth to be rich *hath* an evil eye, and considereth not that poverty shall come upon him.

Pro 28:23 He that rebuketh a man afterwards shall find more favour than he that flattereth with the tongue.

Pro 28:24 Whoso robbeth his father or his mother, and saith, *It is* no transgression; the same *is* the companion of a destroyer.

Pro 28:25 He that is of a proud heart stirreth up strife: but he that putteth his trust in the LORD shall be made fat.

Pro 28:26 He that trusteth in his own heart is a fool: but whoso walketh wisely, he shall be delivered.

Pro 28:27 He that giveth unto the poor shall not lack: but he that hideth his eyes shall have many a curse.

Pro 28:28 When the wicked rise, men hide themselves: but when they perish, the righteous increase.

Proverbs 29

Pro 29:1 He, that being often reproved hardeneth *his* neck, shall suddenly be destroyed, and that without remedy.

Pro 29:2 When the righteous are in authority, the people rejoice: but when the wicked beareth rule, the people mourn.

Pro 29:3 Whoso loveth wisdom rejoiceth his father: but he that keepeth company with harlots spendeth *his* substance.

Pro 29:4 The king by judgment establisheth the land: but he that receiveth gifts overthroweth it.

Pro 29:5 A man that flattereth his neighbour spreadeth a net for his feet.

Pro 29:6 In the transgression of an evil man *there is* a snare: but the righteous doth sing and rejoice.

Pro 29:7 The righteous considereth the cause of the poor: *but* the wicked regardeth not to know *it*.

Pro 29:8 Scornful men bring a city into a snare: but wise *men* turn away wrath.

Pro 29:9 *If* a wise man contendeth with a foolish man, whether he rage or laugh, *there is* no rest.

Pro 29:10 The bloodthirsty hate the upright: but the just seek his soul.

Pro 29:11 A fool uttereth all his mind: but a wise *man* keepeth it in till afterwards.

Pro 29:12 If a ruler hearken to lies, all his servants *are* wicked.

Pro 29:13 The poor and the deceitful man meet together: the LORD lighteneth both their eyes.

Pro 29:14 The king that faithfully judgeth the poor, his throne shall be established for ever.

Pro 29:15 The rod and reproof give wisdom: but a child left *to himself* bringeth his mother to shame.

Pro 29:16 When the wicked are multiplied, transgression increaseth: but the righteous shall see their fall.

Pro 29:17 Correct thy son, and he shall give thee rest; yea, he shall give delight unto thy soul.

Pro 29:18 Where *there is* no vision, the people perish: but he that keepeth the law, happy *is* he.

Pro 29:19 A servant will not be corrected by words: for though he understand he will not answer.

Pro 29:20 Seest thou a man *that is* hasty in his words? *there is* more hope of a fool than of him.

Pro 29:21 He that delicately bringeth up his servant from a child shall have him become *his* son at the length.

Pro 29:22 An angry man stirreth up strife, and a furious man aboundeth in transgression.

Pro 29:23 A man's pride shall bring him low: but honour shall uphold the humble in spirit.

Pro 29:24 Whoso is partner with a thief hateth his own soul: he heareth cursing, and bewrayeth *it* not.

Pro 29:25 The fear of man bringeth a snare: but whoso putteth his trust in the LORD shall be safe.

Pro 29:26 Many seek the ruler's favour; but *every* man's judgment *cometh* from the LORD.

Pro 29:27 An unjust man *is* an abomination to the just: and *he that is* upright in the way *is* abomination to the wicked.

Proverbs 30 and 31

Proverbs 30: "The Words of Agur"

Pro 30:1 The words of Agur the son of Jakeh, *even* the prophecy: the man spake unto Ithiel, even unto Ithiel and Ucal,

Pro 30:2 Surely I *am* more brutish than *any* man, and have not the understanding of a man.

Pro 30:3 I neither learned wisdom, nor have the knowledge of the holy.

Pro 30:4 Who hath ascended up into heaven, or descended? who hath gathered the wind in his fists? who hath bound the waters in a garment? who hath established all the ends of the earth? what *is* his name, and what *is* his son's name, if thou canst tell?

Pro 30:5 Every word of God *is* pure: he *is* a shield unto them that put their trust in him.

Pro 30:6 Add thou not unto his words, lest he reprove thee, and thou be found a liar.

Pro 30:7 Two *things* have I required of thee; deny me *them* not before I die:

Pro 30:8 Remove far from me vanity and lies: give me neither poverty nor riches; feed me with food convenient for me:

Pro 30:9 Lest I be full, and deny *thee*, and say, Who *is* the LORD? or lest I be poor, and steal, and take the name of my God *in vain*.

Pro 30:10 Accuse not a servant unto his master, lest he curse thee, and thou be found guilty.

Pro 30:11 *There is* a generation *that* curseth their father, and doth not bless their mother.

Pro 30:12 *There is* a generation *that are* pure in their own eyes, and *yet* is not washed from their filthiness.

Pro 30:13 *There is* a generation, O how lofty are their eyes! and their eyelids are lifted up.

Pro 30:14 *There is* a generation, whose teeth *are as* swords, and their jaw teeth *as* knives, to devour the poor from off the earth, and the needy from *among* men.

Pro 30:15 The horseleach hath two daughters, *crying*, Give, give. There are three *things that* are never satisfied, *yea*, four *things* say not, It *is* enough:

Pro 30:16 The grave; and the barren womb; the earth *that* is not filled with water; and the fire *that* saith not, It is enough.

Pro 30:17 The eye *that* mocketh at *his* father, and despiseth to obey *his* mother, the ravens of the valley shall pick it out, and the young eagles shall eat it.

Pro 30:18 There be three *things which* are too wonderful for me, yea, four which I know not:

Pro 30:19 The way of an eagle in the air; the way of a serpent upon a rock; the way of a ship in the midst of the sea; and the way of a man with a maid.

Pro 30:20 Such *is* the way of an adulterous woman; she eateth, and wipeth her mouth, and saith, I have done no wickedness.

Pro 30:21 For three *things* the earth is disquieted, and for four *which* it cannot bear:

Pro 30:22 For a servant when he reigneth; and a fool when he is filled with meat;

Pro 30:23 For an odious *woman* when she is married; and an handmaid that is heir to her mistress.

Pro 30:24 There be four *things which are* little upon the earth, but they *are* exceeding wise:

Pro 30:25 The ants *are* a people not strong, yet they prepare their meat in the summer;

Pro 30:26 The conies *are but* a feeble folk, yet make they their houses in the rocks;

Pro 30:27 The locusts have no king, yet go they forth all of them by bands;

Pro 30:28 The spider taketh hold with her hands, and is in kings' palaces.

Pro 30:29 There be three *things* which go well, yea, four are comely in going:

Pro 30:30 A lion *which is* strongest among beasts, and turneth not away for any;

Pro 30:31 A greyhound; an he goat also; and a king, against whom *there is* no rising up.

Pro 30:32 If thou hast done foolishly in lifting up thyself, or if thou hast thought evil, *lay* thine hand upon thy mouth.

Pro 30:33 Surely the churning of milk bringeth forth butter, and the wringing of the nose bringeth forth blood: so the forcing of wrath bringeth forth strife.

Proverbs 31:1 through 31:9: "The Words of King Lemuel of Massa, Which his Mother Taught Him"

Pro 31:1 The words of king Lemuel, the prophecy that his mother taught him.

Pro 31:2 What, my son? and what, the son of my womb? and what, the son of my vows?

Pro 31:3 Give not thy strength unto women, nor thy ways to that which destroyeth kings.

Pro 31:4 *It is* not for kings, O Lemuel, *it is* not for kings to drink wine; nor for princes strong drink:

Pro 31:5 Lest they drink, and forget the law, and pervert the judgment of any of the afflicted.

Pro 31:6 Give strong drink unto him that is ready to perish, and wine unto those that be of heavy hearts.

Pro 31:7 Let him drink, and forget his poverty, and remember his misery no more.

Pro 31:8 Open thy mouth for the dumb in the cause of all such as are appointed to destruction.

Pro 31:9 Open thy mouth, judge righteously, and plead the cause of the poor and needy.

Proverb 31:10 through 31: The ideal wise woman (elsewhere called "the woman of substance")

Pro 31:10 Who can find a virtuous woman? for her price *is* far above rubies.

Pro 31:11 The heart of her husband doth safely trust in her, so that he shall have no need of spoil.

Pro 31:12 She will do him good and not evil all the days of her life.

Pro 31:13 She seeketh wool, and flax, and worketh willingly with her hands.

Pro 31:14 She is like the merchants' ships; she bringeth her food from afar.

Pro 31:15 She riseth also while it is yet night, and giveth meat to her household, and a portion to her maidens.

Pro 31:16 She considereth a field, and buyeth it: with the fruit of her hands she planteth a vineyard.

Pro 31:17 She girdeth her loins with strength, and strengtheneth her arms.

Pro 31:18 She perceiveth that her merchandise *is* good: her candle goeth not out by night.

Pro 31:19 She layeth her hands to the spindle, and her hands hold the distaff.

Pro 31:20 She stretcheth out her hand to the poor; yea, she reacheth forth her hands to the needy.

Pro 31:21 She is not afraid of the snow for her household: for all her household *are* clothed with scarlet.

Pro 31:22 She maketh herself coverings of tapestry; her clothing *is* silk and purple.

Pro 31:23 Her husband is known in the gates, when he sitteth among the elders of the land.

Pro 31:24 She maketh fine linen, and selleth *it;* and delivereth girdles unto the merchant.

Pro 31:25 Strength and honour *are* her clothing; and she shall rejoice in time to come.

Pro 31:26 She openeth her mouth with wisdom; and in her tongue *is* the law of kindness.

Pro 31:27 She looketh well to the ways of her household, and eateth not the bread of idleness.

Pro 31:28 Her children arise up, and call her blessed; her husband *also,* and he praiseth her.

Pro 31:29 Many daughters have done virtuously, but thou excellest them all.
Pro 31:30 Favour *is* deceitful, and beauty *is* vain: *but* a woman *that* feareth the LORD, she shall be praised.
Pro 31:31 Give her of the fruit of her hands; and let her own works praise her in the gates.

SONGS OF SONGS, OR SONGS OF SOLOMON

A variety of explanations can be identified as to the meaning of this Judeo – Christian Bible Book, which is thought to have been authored by King Solomon.

I am persuaded the assessment by some early Hebrew and Christian scholars provides the best explanation. These scholars seems to have maintained that this love story symbolizes the caring relationship that is the love of God for humankind; and the capability in men for loving others *(maybe even divine, and agape love)* that is within the human heart *(perhaps, one of the attributes of God placed there by God from the time He breathed into Adam, and Adam became a living soul? See Genesis 2:7; and "The Kinsman Redeemer" paragraph in the "Definition & Figures" section.*

Present day Bible Researcher's have much to say about "Agape Love", which is commonly referred to as the "God kind of love"! But I am persuaded Paul the Apostle describes it best! Refer to the "Agape Love" paragraph in the "Definitions & Figures" section).

But, it is also undeniable that these songs portray not only love, but the sensuous, and may be even mystical quality of erotic human desire(s), *which we know is associated with procreation commanded of God (Genesis 1:28 and 9:1)*!

And so we have witness of, "Expressions of Natural Human Passions under Approval of the LORD God for Procreation; and Qualified Acceptable Pleasures between the only two (2) Sex Genders" the LORD God of Creation approves of!

However, these songs in no way addresses any of the pitfalls that so often accompany unbridled human passions that ends with sin!

Thus, we must look to other instructions from the Judeo – Christian Scriptures, which command right behavior that is pleasing before our LORD God the Creator; and honestly reject making-up behavior(s) that seems righteous to us (from the point of view of men).

Behold, I have given him *(Jesus for certain, and perhaps David too?) for* a witness to the people, a leader and commander to the people.
Behold, thou shalt call a nation *that* thou knowest not, and nations *that* knew not thee shall run unto thee *(Judah of Israel?)* because of the LORD thy God, and for the Holy One of Israel *(Jesus)*; for he hath glorified thee *(Judah of Israel?)*.
Seek ye the LORD while he may be found, call ye upon him while he is near:
Let the wicked forsake his way, and the unrighteous man his thoughts: and let him return unto the LORD, and he will have mercy upon him; and to our God, for he will abundantly pardon.
For my thoughts *are* not your thoughts, neither *are* your ways my ways, saith the LORD.
For *as* the heavens are higher than the earth, so are my ways higher than your ways, and my thoughts than your thoughts.
For as the rain cometh down, and the snow from heaven, and returneth not thither, but watereth the earth, and maketh it bring forth and bud, that it may give seed to the sower, and bread to the eater:
So shall my word be that goeth forth out of my mouth: it shall not return unto me void, but it shall accomplish that which I please, and it shall prosper *in the thing* whereto I sent it.
Isaiah 55:4 through 55:11

According to this study we have determined that there are three (3) personalities participating in the songs, as follows:

The Virgin's Response; The King's Response, and The Daughters of Jerusalem Response.

Son 1:1 The song of songs, which *is* Solomon's.

THE FIRST SONG

The Virgin's Response
Son 1:2 Let him kiss me with the kisses of his mouth: for thy love *is* better than wine.
Son 1:3 Because of the savour of thy good ointments thy name *is as* ointment poured forth, therefore do the virgins love thee.
Son 1:4 Draw me, we will run after thee: the king hath brought me into his chambers: we will be glad and rejoice in thee, we will remember thy love more than wine: the upright love thee.
Son 1:5 I *am* black, but comely *(or pleasant to look at)*, O ye daughters of Jerusalem, as *(black as?)* the tents of Kedar, as the curtains of Solomon *(am I?)*.
Son 1:6 Look not upon me, because I *am* black, because the sun hath looked upon me: my mother's children were angry with me; they made me the keeper of the vineyards; *but* mine own vineyard have I not kept.
Son 1:7 Tell me, O thou whom my soul loveth, where thou feedest, where thou makest *thy flock* to rest at noon: for why should I be as one that turneth aside by the flocks of thy companions?

The King's Response
Son 1:8 If thou know not *(where I rest at noon?)*, O thou fairest among women, go thy way forth by the footsteps *(or sounding?)* of the flock, and feed thy kids beside the shepherds' tents.
Son 1:9 I have compared thee, O my love, to a company of horses in Pharaoh's chariots.
Son 1:10 Thy cheeks are comely *(or pleasant to look at)* with rows *of jewels*, thy neck with chains *of gold*.
Son 1:11 We will make thee borders of gold with studs of silver.

The Virgin's Response

Son 1:12 While the king *sitteth* at his table, my spikenard *(or perfume)* sendeth forth the smell thereof.

Son 1:13 A bundle of myrrh *(or incense) is* my wellbeloved unto me; he shall lie all night betwixt my breasts.

Son 1:14 My beloved *is* unto me *as* a cluster of camphire *(or pleasant smell of spices?)* in the vineyards of Engedi.

The King's Response

Son 1:15 Behold, thou *art* fair, my love; behold, thou *art* fair; thou *hast* doves' eyes.

Son 1:16 Behold, thou *art* fair, my beloved, yea, pleasant: also our bed *is* green *(alive\ fresh?)*.

Son 1:17 The beams of our house *are* cedar, *and* our rafters of fir.

A Figure of Jesus?

Son 2:1 I *am* the rose of Sharon, *and* the lily of the valleys *(these **beautiful flowers often grow even in unfavorable environments; similar to the meaning of, "a root out of a dry ground"? Refer Isaiah 53:1 and 53:2.)**.

Who hath believed our report? And to whom is the arm *(Messiah, Jesus)* of the LORD revealed?

For he *(the arm of the LORD)* shall grow up before him *(the LORD)* as a tender plant, and as a root out of a dry ground *(**This speaks of the virgin birth of Jesus. In the natural it would take a miracle for a seed to germinate in dry ground; and so the virgin birth of Jesus required conception by the Holy Spirit; thus Jesus was born of a virgin!**)*: he hath no form nor comeliness; and when we shall see him, *there is* no beauty that we should desire him *(he, **Jesus looked like an ordinary man of His day and time**)*.

Isaiah 53:1 and 53:2

Son 2:2 As the lily among thorns, so *is* my love among the daughters *(of Jerusalem?)*.

The Virgin's Response

Son 2:3 As the apple tree among the trees of the wood, so *is* my beloved among the sons. I sat down under his shadow with great delight, and his fruit *was* sweet to my taste.

Son 2:4 He brought me to the banqueting house, and his banner over me *was* love.

Son 2:5 Stay me with flagons *(of drink?)*, comfort me with apples: for I *am* sick of *(or unto)* love.

Son 2:6 His left hand *is* under my head, and his right hand doth embrace me.

Son 2:7 I charge you, O ye daughters of Jerusalem, by the roes, and by the hinds *(a kind of deer)* of the field, that ye stir not up, nor awake *my* love, till he please.

THE SECOND SONG

Son 2:8 The voice of my beloved! behold, he cometh leaping upon the mountains, skipping upon the hills.

Son 2:9 My beloved is like a roe or a young hart: behold, he standeth behind our wall, he looketh forth at the windows, shewing himself through the lattice.

Son 2:10 My beloved spake, and said unto me, Rise up, my love, my fair one, and come away.

The King's Response

Son 2:11 For, lo, the winter is past, the rain is over *and* gone;

Son 2:12 The flowers appear on the earth; the time of the singing *of birds* is come, and the voice of the turtle is heard in our land;

Son 2:13 The fig tree putteth forth her green figs, and the vines *with* the tender grape give a *good* smell. Arise, my love, my fair one, and come away.

Son 2:14 O my dove, *that art* in the clefts of the rock, in the secret *places* of the stairs, let me see thy countenance, let me hear thy voice; for sweet *is* thy voice, and thy countenance *is* comely *(or pleasant to look at)*.

The Virgin's Response
Son 2:15 Take us *(or consider?)* the foxes, the little foxes, that spoil the vines: for our vines *have* tender grapes.
Son 2:16 My beloved *is* mine, and I *am* his: he feedeth among the lilies.
Son 2:17 Until the day break, and the shadows flee away, turn, my beloved, and be thou like a roe or a young hart upon the mountains of Bether.

Son 3:1 By night on my bed I sought him whom my soul loveth: I sought him, but I found him not.
Son 3:2 I will rise now, and go about the city in the streets, and in the broad ways I will seek him whom my soul loveth: I sought him, but I found him not.
Son 3:3 The watchmen that go about the city found me: *to whom I said,* Saw ye him whom my soul loveth?

The Wedding
Son 3:4 *It was* but a little *(while?)* that I passed from them *(the watchmen)*, but I found him whom my soul loveth: I held him, and would not let him go, until I had brought him into my mother's house, and into the chamber of her that conceived me *(this scripture suggests a wedding took place; the King with the Virgin?)*.
Son 3:5 I charge you, O ye daughters of Jerusalem, by the roes, and by the hinds of the field, that ye stir not up, nor awake *my* love, till he please.

THE THIRD SONG

Son 3:6 Who *is* this that cometh out of the wilderness like pillars of smoke, perfumed with myrrh *(or incense)* and frankincense, with all powders of the merchant?
Son 3:7 Behold his bed, which *is* Solomon's; threescore *(60)* valiant men *are* about it, of the valiant of Israel.

Son 3:8 They all hold swords, *being* expert in war: every man *hath* his sword upon his thigh because of fear in the night.

Son 3:9 King Solomon made himself a chariot of the wood of Lebanon.

Son 3:10 He made the pillars thereof *of* silver, the bottom thereof *of* gold, the covering of it *of* purple, the midst thereof being paved *with* love, for the daughters of Jerusalem.

Son 3:11 Go forth, O ye daughters of Zion, and behold king Solomon with the crown wherewith his mother crowned him in the day of his espousals, and in the day of the gladness of his heart.

The King's Response

Son 4:1 Behold, thou *art* fair, my love; behold, thou *art* fair; thou *hast* doves' eyes within thy locks: thy hair *is* as a flock of goats, that appear from mount Gilead.

Son 4:2 Thy teeth *are* like a flock *of sheep that are even* shorn, which came up from the washing; whereof every one bear twins, and none *is* barren among them.

Son 4:3 Thy lips *are* like a thread of scarlet, and thy speech *is* comely: thy temples *are* like a piece of a pomegranate within thy locks.

Son 4:4 Thy neck *is* like the tower of David builded for an armoury, whereon there hang a thousand *(1000)* bucklers, all shields of mighty men.

Son 4:5 Thy two *(2)* breasts *are* like two *(2)* young roes that are twins, which feed among the lilies.

Son 4:6 Until the day break, and the shadows flee away, I will get me to the mountain of myrrh *(or incense)*, and to the hill of frankincense.

Son 4:7 Thou *art* all fair, my love; *there is* no spot *(or flaw?)* in thee.

Son 4:8 Come with me from Lebanon, *my* spouse, with me from Lebanon: look from the top of Amana, from the top of Shenir and Hermon, from the lions' dens, from the mountains of the leopards.

Son 4:9 Thou hast ravished my heart, my sister, *my* spouse; thou hast ravished my heart with one of thine eyes, with one chain of thy neck.

Son 4:10 How fair is thy love, my sister, *my* spouse! how much better is thy love than wine! and the smell of thine ointments than all spices!

Son 4:11 Thy lips, O *my* spouse, drop *as* the honeycomb: honey and milk *are* under thy tongue; and the smell of thy garments *is* like the smell of Lebanon.

Son 4:12 A garden inclosed *is* my sister, *my* spouse; a spring shut up, a fountain sealed.

The Virgin which became the Spouse in Song 3, Verse 4 Response

Son 4:13 Thy plants *are* an orchard of pomegranates, with pleasant fruits; camphire *(or pleasant smell of spices?)*, with spikenard,

Son 4:14 Spikenard and saffron; calamus *(a perfume ingredient)* and cinnamon, with all trees of frankincense; myrrh *(or incense)* and aloes, with all the chief spices:

Son 4:15 A fountain of gardens, a well of living waters, and streams from Lebanon.

Son 4:16 Awake, O north wind; and come, thou south; blow upon my garden, *that* the spices thereof may flow out. Let my beloved come into his garden, and eat his pleasant fruits.

The King's Response

Son 5:1 I am come into my garden, my sister, *my* spouse: I have gathered my myrrh *(or incense)* with my spice; I have eaten my honeycomb with my honey; I have drunk my wine with my milk: eat, O friends; drink, yea, drink abundantly, O beloved.

THE FOUTH SONG

The Virgin which became the Spouse in Song 3, Verse 4 Response

Son 5:2 I sleep, but my heart waketh: *it is* the voice of my beloved that knocketh, *saying,* Open to me, my sister, my love, my dove, my undefiled: for my head is filled with dew, *and* my locks with the drops of the night.

Son 5:3 I have put off my coat; how shall I put it on? I have washed my feet; how shall I defile them?

Son 5:4 My beloved put in his hand by the hole *of the door,* and my bowels were moved for him.

Son 5:5 I rose up to open to my beloved; and my hands dropped *with* myrrh *(or incense)*, and my fingers *with* sweet smelling myrrh *(or incense)*, upon the handles of the lock.

Son 5:6 I opened to my beloved; but my beloved had withdrawn himself, *and* was gone: my soul failed when he spake: I sought him, but I could not find him; I called him, but he gave me no answer.

Son 5:7 The watchmen that went about the city found me, they smote me, they wounded me; the keepers of the walls took away my veil from me.

Son 5:8 I charge you, O daughters of Jerusalem, if ye find my beloved, that ye tell him, that I *am* sick of *(or unto)* love.

The Daughters of Jerusalem Response

Son 5:9 What *is* thy beloved more than *another* beloved, O thou fairest among women? what *is* thy beloved more than *another* beloved, that thou dost so charge us?

The Virgin which became the Spouse in Song 3, Verse 4 Response

Son 5:10 My beloved *is* white and ruddy, the chiefest among ten *(10, 000)* thousand.

Son 5:11 His head *is as* the most fine gold, his locks *are* bushy, *and* black as a raven.

Son 5:12 His eyes *are* as *the eyes* of doves by the rivers of waters, washed with milk, *and* fitly set.

Son 5:13 His cheeks *are* as a bed of spices, *as* sweet flowers: his lips *like* lilies, dropping sweet smelling myrrh *(or incense)*.

Son 5:14 His hands *are as* gold rings set with the beryl: his belly *is as* bright ivory overlaid *with* sapphires.

Son 5:15 His legs *are as* pillars of marble, set upon sockets of fine gold: his countenance *is* as Lebanon, excellent as the cedars.

Son 5:16 His mouth *is* most sweet: yea, he *is* altogether lovely. This *is* my beloved, and this *is* my friend, O daughters of Jerusalem.

The Daughters of Jerusalem Response
Son 6:1 Whither is thy beloved gone, O thou fairest among women? whither is thy beloved turned aside? that we may seek him with thee.

The Virgin which became the Spouse in Song 3, Verse 4 Response
Son 6:2 My beloved is gone down into his garden, to the beds of spices, to feed in the gardens, and to gather lilies.
Son 6:3 I *am* my beloved's, and my beloved *is* mine: he feedeth among the lilies.

THE FIFTH SONG

The King's Response
Son 6:4 Thou *art* beautiful, O my love, as Tirzah, comely *(or pleasant to look at)* as Jerusalem, terrible *(or awesome)* as *an army* with banners.
Son 6:5 Turn away thine eyes from me, for they have overcome me: thy hair *is* as a flock of goats that appear from Gilead.
Son 6:6 Thy teeth *are* as a flock of sheep which go up from the washing, whereof every one beareth twins, and *there is* not one barren among them.
Son 6:7 As a piece of a pomegranate *are* thy temples within thy locks.
Son 6:8 There are threescore *(60)* queens, and fourscore *(80)* concubines, and virgins without number.
Son 6:9 My dove, my undefiled is *but* one *(of them?)*; she *is* the *only* one of her mother, she *is* the choice *one* of her that bare her. The daughters saw her, and blessed her; *yea,* the queens and the concubines, and they praised her.
Son 6:10 Who *is* she *that* looketh forth as the morning, fair as the moon, clear as the sun, *and* terrible *(or awesome)* as *an army* with banners?
Son 6:11 I went down into the garden of nuts to see the fruits of the valley, *and* to see whether the vine flourished, *and* the pomegranates budded.
Son 6:12 Or ever I was aware, my soul made me *like* the chariots of Amminadib.

Son 6:13 Return, return, O Shulamite; return, return, that we may look upon thee. What will ye see in the Shulamite? As it were the company of two *(2)* armies.

Son 7:1 How beautiful are thy feet with shoes, O prince's daughter! the joints of thy thighs *are* like jewels, the work of the hands of a cunning workman.
Son 7:2 Thy navel *is like* a round goblet, *which* wanteth not liquor: thy belly *is like* an heap of wheat set about with lilies.
Son 7:3 Thy two *(2)* breasts *are* like two *(2)* young roes *that are* twins.

The Virgin which became the Spouse in Song 3, Verse 4 Response
Son 7:4 Thy neck *is* as a tower of ivory; thine eyes *like* the fishpools in Heshbon, by the gate of Bathrabbim: thy nose *is* as the tower of Lebanon which looketh toward Damascus.
Son 7:5 Thine head upon thee *is* like Carmel, and the hair of thine head like purple; the king *is* held in the galleries.
Son 7:6 How fair and how pleasant art thou, O love, for delights!
Son 7:7 This thy stature is like to a palm tree, and thy breasts to clusters *of grapes.*
Son 7:8 I said, I will go up to the palm tree, I will take hold of the boughs thereof: now also thy breasts shall be as clusters of the vine, and the smell of thy nose like apples;
Son 7:9 And the roof of thy mouth like the best wine for my beloved, that goeth *down* sweetly, causing the lips of those that are asleep to speak.
Son 7:10 I *am* my beloved's, and his desire *is* toward me.
Son 7:11 Come, my beloved, let us go forth into the field; let us lodge in the villages.
Son 7:12 Let us get up early to the vineyards; let us see if the vine flourish, *whether* the tender grape appear, *and* the pomegranates bud forth: there will I give thee my loves.
Son 7:13 The mandrakes give a smell, and at our gates *are* all manner of pleasant *fruits,* new and old, *which* I have laid up for thee, O my beloved.

Son 8:1 O that thou *wert* as my brother, that sucked the breasts of my mother! *when* I should find thee without, I would kiss thee; yea, I should not be despised.

Son 8:2 I would lead thee, *and* bring thee into my mother's house, *who* would instruct me: I would cause thee to drink of spiced wine of the juice of my pomegranate.

Son 8:3 His left hand *should be* under my head, and his right hand should embrace me.

Son 8:4 I charge you, O daughters of Jerusalem, that ye stir not up, nor awake *my* love, until he please.

THE SIXTH SONG

The Daughters of Jerusalem Response

Son 8:5 Who *is* this that cometh up from the wilderness, leaning upon her beloved? I raised thee up under the apple tree: there thy mother brought thee forth: there she brought thee forth *that* bare thee.

Son 8:6 Set me as a seal upon thine heart, as a seal upon thine arm: for love *is* strong as death; jealousy *is* cruel as the grave: the coals thereof *are* coals of fire, *which hath a* most vehement flame.

Son 8:7 Many waters cannot quench love, neither can the floods drown it: if *a* man would give all the substance of his house for love, it would utterly be contemned.

Son 8:8 We have a little sister, and she hath no breasts: what shall we do for our sister in the day when she shall be spoken for **(can this mean a girl child is born to the King and the Virgin which became the Spouse in Song 3, Verse 4?)**?

Son 8:9 If she *be* a wall, we will build upon her a palace of silver: and if she *be* a door, we will inclose her with boards of cedar.

The Virgin which became the Spouse in Song 3, Verse 4 Response

Son 8:10 I *am* a wall, and my breasts like towers: then was I in his eyes as one that found favour.

Son 8:11 Solomon had a vineyard at Baalhamon; he let out the vineyard unto keepers; every one for the fruit thereof was to bring a thousand *(1000) pieces* of silver.

Son 8:12 My vineyard, which *is* mine, *is* before me: thou, O Solomon, *must have* a thousand *(1000)*, and those that keep the fruit thereof two *(200)* hundred.

Son 8:13 Thou that dwellest in the gardens, the companions hearken to thy voice: cause me to hear *it*.

Son 8:14 Make haste, my beloved, and be thou like to a roe or to a young hart upon the mountains of spices.

ECCLESIASTES

During the study of this Book of Ecclesiastes, I kept looking for scriptures where Solomon abandoned God using specific declaration(s)! I could not identify any!

However, like anyone else it seems discouragement was something Solomon wrestled with too, later in his life. And I believe the issue of "vanity" and how he viewed it might have been a testimony of his discouragement!

I am also persuaded it is not clear from these writings that Solomon lost full sight of his God, and became hopelessly bogged down in false god, idol worship, and weariness of day-to-day routine living? But we do see from other Bible scripture that he disobeyed the LORD on this wise of (1 Kings Chapter 11)!

The LORD God had commanded him not to take wives and\ or concubines from foreign; or heathen nations (or women outside of Israel!), because they (and their false gods and idol worship) would draw him away from serving the God of Abraham, Isaac, and Jacob; the True God of Creation!

Our God of the Judeo – Christian Bible is the only Living God, and He promises His servants life that is everlasting!

Therefore, the question arises, "how could Solomon conclude vanity awaited him, except for having lost sizable convictions of his faith (perhaps, not fully understanding, or experienced serious discouragement for a time) in God and His promises?"

Thus, Solomon had so much stuff; experienced so many things that maybe; for a time he replaced God as first place in his life and living!

It seems he begin to believe nothing else could be added to life, even if he was given more life (including life forever)?

And so, did the things; stuff; abundant experiences; and false gods take hold of Solomon, and replaced the, "True God of Creation; the God of his Fathers" in his every day existence, for a time as he approached the end of his earthly days?

We do not know for certain whether Solomon recovered? And this Bible student is left wondering if 2 Samuel Chapter 7:13 through 7:17 saved every, "Judah of Israel individual" from their iniquity as was described concerning David, below:

Jacob, or Israel has favor with the LORD God, but God never withheld judgment from dealing with the Nation, "Israel" according to their iniquity, when it was required!

However; we know from other prophetic studies the final state of "Judah of Israel, the remnant people of God" shall be righteousness forever! But did this save Solomon, "the individual"; or any other king in the linage of David; or any other Judah of Israel citizen that abandoned God, and did not return?

2 Sa 7:13 He *(David and his seed)* shall build an house for my name, and I will stablish the throne of his kingdom for ever.

Did these next two verses (2 Samuel 7:14 and 7:15) save Solomon, and other Old Testament citizens of Israel?

2 Sa 7:14 I will be his father, and he shall be my son. If he commit iniquity, I will chasten him with the rod of men, and with the stripes of the children of men:
2 Sa 7:15 But my mercy shall not depart away from him, as I took *it* from Saul, whom I put away before thee *(from being king?)*.

2 Sa 7:16 And thine house and thy kingdom shall be established for ever before thee: thy throne shall be established for ever *(Refer to, "Thy Throne Forever" in the "Definitions & Figures")* section.

2 Sa 7:17 According to all these words, and according to all this vision *(and prophecy!)*, so did Nathan *(the prophet)* speak unto David.

The LORD God Established Cycles of Events in His Creation

Even from the time of Judeo – Christian Bible writings provided in the Book of Job Chapters 40 and 41 unfathomable mysteries of the Planet are spoken of! And yours truly is one persuaded by that witness; which is "the LORD God has everything, everywhere under His authority and subjection"! Refer to the paragraphs, "Job Chapters 40 and 41", "Behemoth" and "Leviathan" in the "Definition & Figures" section.

And so, in my mind King Solomon makes quite an additional impact to Job's revelations as he (Solomon) describe how God manages creation's processes, and where His human creature "man", of Planet Earth fit into that Creation!

Thus, it is obvious the Judeo – Christian Bible Scriptures declared a cyclic behavior for creation, long, long before the present day global warming; climate change debates. And even most devout Church goers shall be surprised to realize that regeneration (or the Born Again experience) of the human race is included with the Cycles of Events of Creation (Revelation 21:5 through 21:7), to them that <u>believe</u> according to John 3:16?

And we can add to this witness, the words the LORD God declared by the prophet Isaiah, according to the Book of Isaiah, Chapter 55:8 through 55:11!

Isa 55:8 For my thoughts *are* not your thoughts, neither *are* your ways my ways, saith the LORD.

Isa 55:9 For as the heavens are higher than the earth, so are my ways higher than your ways, and my thoughts than your thoughts.

Isa 55:10 For as the rain cometh down, and the snow from heaven, and returneth not thither, but watereth the earth, and maketh it bring forth and bud, that it may give seed to the sower, and bread to the eater:

Isa 55:11 So shall my word be that goeth forth out of my mouth: it shall not return unto me void, but it shall accomplish that which I please, and it shall prosper in the thing whereto I sent it.

And so, nothing of the Creation shall run off its rails (or fall apart completely) unless the LORD God intend and allows it!

However, those not convinced of this shall always put forth efforts to fix, "as they see it, the mistakes in the spontaneously self created, Creation", because of their lack of trust in anything; especially the true God of Heaven!

I am persuaded King Solomon's reasoning bear these truths out in this Book of Ecclesiastes as follows:

Ecclesiastes Chapter 1

Ecc 1:1 The words of the Preacher, the son of David, king in Jerusalem.

Ecc 1:2 Vanity of vanities, saith the Preacher, vanity of vanities; all *is* vanity.

Ecc 1:3 What profit *(or gain)* hath a man of all his labour which he taketh under the sun?

Ecc 1:4 *One* generation passeth away, and *another* generation cometh: but the earth abideth for ever.

Ecc 1:5 The sun also ariseth, and the sun goeth down, and hasteth to his place where he arose.

Ecc 1:6 The wind goeth toward the south, and turneth about unto the north; it *(the wind)* whirleth about continually, and the wind returneth again according to his circuits *(or path of a previous journey in times)*.

Ecc 1:7 All the rivers run into the sea; yet the sea *is* not full; unto the place from whence the rivers come, thither they return again *(those of science would explain this as the process of water evaporating into the atmosphere; cooling the "evaporated water filled air" (or condensing the evaporated water) and it fall to the earth again as rain, snow, or ice. And the cycle repeats again and again …!).*

Ecc 1:8 All things *are* full of labour; man cannot utter *(or name all of) it:* the eye is not satisfied with seeing, nor the ear filled with hearing.

Ecc 1:9 The thing that hath been, it *is that* which shall be; and that which is done *is* that which shall be done: and *there is* no new *thing* under the sun *(and methods of doing things may change; but the seeing, hearing, and making use of, remains the requirement?).*

Ecc 1:10 *(Concerning the Creation,)* Is there *any* thing whereof it may be said, See, this *is* new? it hath been already of old time, which was before us.

Ecc 1:11 *There is* no remembrance of former *things;* neither shall there be *any* remembrance of *things* that are to come with *those* that shall come after *(and given enough time people and events are forgotten, even recorded things?).*

Ecc 1:12 I the Preacher was king over Israel in Jerusalem.

Ecc 1:13 And I gave my heart to seek and search out by wisdom concerning all *things* that are done under heaven: this sore *(or agonizing?)* travail hath God given to the sons of man to be exercised *(or busied)* therewith.

The Creation of Adam

And God said, Let us make man in our image, after our likeness: and let them have dominion over the fish of the sea, and over the fowl of the air, and over the cattle, and over all the earth, and over every creeping thing that creepeth upon the earth.

So God created man in his *own* image, in the image of God created he him; male and female created he them *(Refer to, "The Kinsman Redeemer" in the "Definitions & Figures")* section.

And God blessed them *(male and female)*, and God said unto them, Be fruitful, and multiply, and replenish the earth, and subdue it: and have dominion over the fish of the sea, and over the fowl of the air, and over every living thing that moveth upon the earth *(obviously, the Lord God knew two males together, or two females together would have no fruitfulness to replenish the earth! Thus, the race would cease, and the earth would not be replenished, nor subdued; and this mandate commanded of God would be nullified!)*

But the LORD God declared by the prophet Isaiah, the following:

Isa 55:9 For *as* the heavens are higher than the earth, so are my ways higher than your ways, and my thoughts than your thoughts.
Isa 55:10 For as the rain cometh down, and the snow from heaven, and returneth not thither, but watereth the earth, and maketh it bring forth and bud, that it may give seed to the sower, and bread to the eater:
Isa 55:11 So shall my word be that goeth forth out of my mouth: it shall not return unto me void, but it shall accomplish that which I please, and it shall prosper *in the thing* whereto I sent it.*).*

And God said, Behold, I have given you every herb bearing seed, which *is* upon the face of all the earth, and every tree, in the which *is* the fruit of a tree yielding seed; to you it shall be for meat *(the understanding here is that God created every living thing with its own seed).*
And to every beast of the earth, and to every fowl of the air, and to every thing that creepeth upon the earth, wherein *there is* life, *I have given* every green herb for meat: and it was so.
And God saw every thing that he had made, and, behold, *it was* very good. And the evening and the morning were the sixth *(6th)* day. Genesis 1:26 through 1:31

Solomon did not Always Consult the LORD God

This is a time Solomon communed (or consulted) with his own heart, but it seems he forgot to consult with the LORD God (whom nothing is too hard for Him to do; Isaiah 40:3 through 40:8 speak to the issues Solomon addresses here in Ecclesiastes 1:14 & 1:15. And so without consulting the LORD God, Solomon's wisdom was indeed greater than any other man of his day, but it is not equal with the LORD God and what he can bring to pass!):

Ecc 1:14 I *(Solomon)* have seen all the works that are done under the sun; and, behold, all *is* vanity and vexation of spirit.

Ecc 1:15 *That which is* crooked cannot be made straight: and that which is wanting *(missing, or fallen short of being enough)* cannot be numbered *(made up, or accounted for?)*.

Ecc 1:16 I communed with mine own heart, saying, Lo, I am come to great estate *(or authority and possessions)*, and have gotten more wisdom than all *they* that have been before me in Jerusalem: yea, my heart had great experience of wisdom and knowledge.

Ecc 1:17 And I gave my heart to know wisdom, and to know madness and folly: I perceived that this also is vexation of spirit.

Ecc 1:18 For in much wisdom *is* much grief: and he that increaseth knowledge increaseth sorrow.

Ecclesiastes Chapter 2

Ecc 2:1 I said in mine heart, Go to now, I will prove thee with mirth *(or merriment)*, therefore enjoy pleasure: and, behold, this also *is* vanity.

Ecc 2:2 I said of laughter, *It is* mad: and of mirth, What doeth it *(or this is vanity too!)*?

Ecc 2:3 I sought in mine heart to give myself unto wine, yet acquainting mine heart with wisdom; and to lay hold on folly, till I might see what *was* that good for the sons of men, which they should do under the heaven all the days of their life.

Ecc 2:4 I made me great works; I builded me houses; I planted me vineyards:

Ecc 2:5 I made me gardens and orchards, and I planted trees in them of all *kind of* fruits:

Ecc 2:6 I made me pools of water, to water therewith the wood that bringeth forth trees:

Ecc 2:7 I got *me* servants and maidens, and had servants born in my house; also I had great possessions of great and small cattle above all that were in Jerusalem before me:

Ecc 2:8 I gathered me also silver and gold, and the peculiar treasure of kings and of the provinces: I gat me men singers and women singers, and the delights of the sons of men, *as* musical instruments, and that of all sorts.

Ecc 2:9 So I was great, and increased more than all that were before me in Jerusalem: also my wisdom remained with me.

Ecc 2:10 And whatsoever mine eyes desired I kept not from them, I withheld not my heart from any joy; for my heart rejoiced in all my labour: and this was my portion of all my labour.

Ecc 2:11 Then I looked on all the works that my hands had wrought, and on the labour that I had laboured to do: and, behold, all *was* vanity and vexation of spirit, and *there was* no profit under the sun.

Ecc 2:12 And I turned myself to behold wisdom, and madness, and folly: for what *can* the man *do* that cometh after the king? *even* that which hath been already done.

Ecc 2:13 Then I saw that wisdom excelleth folly, as far as light excelleth darkness.

Ecc 2:14 The wise man's eyes *are* in his head; but the fool walketh in darkness: and I myself perceived also that one event happeneth to them all *(or death comes for all?)*.

Ecc 2:15 Then said I in my heart, As it happeneth to the fool, so it happeneth even to me; and why was I then more wise *(or how does wisdom benefit where the case of death is concerned?)*? Then I said in my heart, that this also *is* vanity.

Ecc 2:16 For *there is* no remembrance of the wise more than of the fool for ever; seeing that which now *is* in the days to come shall all be forgotten. And how dieth the wise *man?* as the fool.

Ecc 2:17 Therefore I hated life; because the work that is wrought under the sun *is* grievous unto me: for all *is* vanity and vexation of spirit.

Ecc 2:18 Yea, I hated all my labour *(or gain?)* which I had taken under the sun: because I should leave it unto the man that shall be after me.

Ecc 2:19 And who knoweth whether he *(after me)* shall be a wise *man* or a fool? yet shall he have rule over all my labour *(gain?)* wherein I have laboured, and wherein I have shewed myself wise under the sun. This *is* also vanity.

Ecc 2:20 Therefore I went about to cause my heart to despair of all the labour *(gain)* which I took under the sun.

Ecc 2:21 For there is a man whose labour *(or gain?)* *is* in wisdom, and in knowledge, and in equity; yet to a man that hath not laboured therein *(or gained in wisdom, and in knowledge)* shall he leave it *for* his portion. This also *is* vanity and a great evil **(when one having not left any gain in wisdom, and in knowledge?)**.

Ecc 2:22 For what hath man of all his labour, and of the vexation of his heart, wherein he hath laboured under the sun?

Ecc 2:23 For all his days *are* sorrows, and his travail grief; yea, his heart taketh not rest *(because of worry?)* in the night. This is also vanity.

But is There Any Gain from Labor Absent of the LORD God?

Ecc 2:24 *There is* nothing better for a man, *than* that he should eat and drink, and *that* he should make his soul enjoy good in his labour. This also I saw, that it *was* from the hand of God.

Ecc 2:25 For who can eat, or who else can hasten *hereunto*, more than I?

Ecc 2:26 For *God* giveth to a man that *is* good in his sight wisdom, and knowledge, and joy: but to the sinner he giveth travail, to gather and to heap up, that he may give to *him that is* good before God. This also *is* vanity and vexation of spirit *(because everyone passes their labor (good or bad) to those that follow?)*.

Ecclesiastes Chapter 3

A Season and Time for Every Purpose Under Heaven

Ecc 3:1 To every *thing there is* a season, and a time to every purpose under the heaven:

Ecc 3:2 A time to be born, and a time to die; a time to plant, and a time to pluck up *that which is* planted;

Ecc 3:3 A time to kill, and a time to heal; a time to break down, and a time to build up;

Ecc 3:4 A time to weep, and a time to laugh; a time to mourn, and a time to dance;

Ecc 3:5 A time to cast away stones, and a time to gather stones together; a time to embrace, and a time to refrain from embracing;

Ecc 3:6 A time to get, and a time to lose; a time to keep, and a time to cast away;

Ecc 3:7 A time to rend *(or tear apart)*, and a time to sew; a time to keep silence, and a time to speak;

Ecc 3:8 A time to love, and a time to hate; a time of war, and a time of peace.

Ecc 3:9 What profit hath he that worketh in that wherein he laboureth?

Ecc 3:10 I have seen the travail, which God hath given to the sons of men to be exercised in it.

Ecc 3:11 He hath made every *thing* beautiful in his time: also he hath set the world in their heart, so that no man can find out the work that God maketh from the beginning to the end.

Ecc 3:12 I know that *there is* no good in them, but for *a man* to rejoice, and to do good in his life.

Ecc 3:13 And also that every man should eat and drink, and enjoy the good of all his labour, it *is* the gift of God.

Ecc 3:14 I know that, whatsoever God doeth, it shall be for ever: nothing can be put *(or added)* to it, nor any thing taken from it: and God doeth *it*, that *men* should fear before him.

Ecc 3:15 That which hath been is now; and that which is to be hath already been; and God requireth that which is past.

Ecc 3:16 And moreover I saw under the sun the place of judgment, *that* wickedness *was* there; and the place of righteousness, *that* iniquity *was* there.

Ecc 3:17 I said in mine heart, God shall judge the righteous and the wicked: for *there is* a time there for every purpose and for every work.

It Seems Solomon Did Not have the Full Revelation of Salvation?

Ecc 3:18 I said in mine heart concerning the estate of the sons of men, that God might manifest them, and that they might see that they themselves are beasts.

Ecc 3:19 For that which befalleth the sons of men befalleth beasts; even one thing befalleth them: as the one dieth, so dieth the other; yea, they have all one breath; so that a man hath no preeminence above a beast: for all *is* vanity.

Ecc 3:20 All go unto one place; all are of the dust, and all turn to dust again.

Ecc 3:21 Who knoweth the spirit of man that goeth upward, and the spirit of the beast that goeth downward to the earth?

Ecc 3:22 Wherefore I perceive that *there is* nothing better, than that a man should rejoice in his own works; for that *is* his portion: for who shall bring him to see what shall be after him?

Solomon explains that the spirit of man is different than that of the beast! And he knew the flesh of both, man and beast returns to dust! But it seems Solomon did not have full revelation of the "salvation story"; probably, because the full mystery of salvation in Christ Jesus was not revealed until the ministry of Jesus, by Jesus!

Moses, Isaiah, Daniel, and other men of God spoke considerable prophecies about Messiah: Moses identified Him as One like unto himself (Deuteronomy 18:15 through 18:22); others called Him the Son of Man; Isaiah said He is "Emanuel", or God with us; Job said, "I know my Redeemer lives"; the general population of His day referred to Him as, "son of David" ...!

But Jesus filled in, fulfilled, and revealed final details from God of what we should expect; then ascended into heaven again!

This is revealed for us today in the sacrificial salvation "Message of the Cross of Christ Jesus"; which no one had been given total revelation of until Messiah Jesus gave it during His three and one-half (3 ½) year ministry (Refer to Matthew Chapter 12:38 through 12:41; also Luke Chapter 11:29 through 11:31):

Then certain of the scribes and of the Pharisees answered, saying, Master, we would see a sign from thee *(to prove who you say you are?)*.

But he *(Jesus)* answered and said unto them, An evil and adulterous generation seeketh after a sign; and there shall no sign be given to it, but the sign of the prophet Jonas *(who was in the whale's belly three (3) days and three (3) nights)*:

For as Jonas was three *(3)* days and three *(3)* nights in the whale's belly; so shall the Son of man be three *(3)* days and three *(3)* nights in the heart of the earth.

The men of Nineveh shall rise in judgment with this generation, and shall condemn it: because they repented at the preaching of Jonas; and, behold, a greater than Jonas *is* here.

The queen of the south shall rise up in the judgment with this generation, and shall condemn it: for she came from the uttermost parts of the earth to hear the wisdom of Solomon; and, behold, **a greater than Solomon *is* here**.

Matthew 12:38 through 12:42

==================================

BUT ...!

(Vanity has been made of none effect, because life without end is made available to <u>them that believe</u> for forgiveness and redemption by the mercy of God, which is salvation in Christ Jesus our savior! See how Paul the Apostle explains it in 1 Corinthians Chapter 15.)

===========================

1 Corinthians Chapter 15

Paul describes in great detail what good things that are sure to come by Christ Jesus, and these great blessings are accessible to those that have <u>faith</u> in His death, burial, and resurrection for deliverance, salvation, and forgiveness of sin unto eternal life. See Matthew John 3:16, John 14:6, Romans 10:9, and 10:10!

1 Co 15:1 Moreover, brethren, I declare unto you the gospel which I preached unto you, which also ye have received *(or believed, and have faith in)*, and wherein ye stand;

> By which also ye are saved *(from the wrath of God because of our sin)*, if ye keep in memory *(or not forget/ give up/ turn away from your faith)* what I preached unto you, unless ye have believed in vain *(or, if we abandon faith now of Christ Jesus; previous faith efforts become vain\ useless)*.
> For I delivered unto you first *(1st)* of all that which I also received, how that Christ died for our sins according to the scriptures;
> And that he was buried, and that he rose again the third *(3rd)* day according to the scriptures *(Old Testament Prophecy, and New Testament witness of fulfilling; praise the LORD God)*:
> And that he *(Jesus)* was seen of Cephas *(Peter)*, then of the twelve *(12 apostles after His resurrection)*:
> After that, he *(Jesus)* was seen of above five hundred *(5, 000)* brethren at once; of whom the greater part remain unto this present *(day)*, but some are fallen asleep *(or have died)*.
> After that, he *(Jesus)* was seen of James *(the Apostle)*; then of all the apostles.
> And last of all he *(Jesus)* was seen of me *(Paul, on the Damascus Road)* also, as of one *(I, Paul)* born out of due time *(or after His ascension into heaven)*.
> For I am the least of the apostles, that am not meet *(counted/ deserving)* to be called an apostle, because I persecuted the church of God.

But by the grace of God I am what I am: and his grace which *was bestowed* upon me was not in vain; but I laboured more abundantly than they all: yet not I, but the grace of God which was with me.

Therefore whether *it were* I or they *(other followers of Christ Jesus that labored)*, so we preach, and so ye believed *(that Jesus is raised from the dead for deliverance, salvation, forgiveness of sin unto eternal life to them that believe)*.

1 Corinthians 15:1 through 15:11

What if some believe there is no resurrection of the dead?

Now if Christ be preached that he rose from the dead, how say some among you that there is no resurrection of the dead *(is it not because of their unbelief)*?

But if there be no resurrection of the dead, then is Christ not risen:

And if Christ be not risen, then *is* our preaching vain, and your faith *is* also vain.

Yea, and we are found false witnesses of God; because we have testified of God *(to others)* that he *(God)* raised up Christ *(from the dead)*: whom he raised not up, if so be that the dead rise not.

For if the dead rise not, then is not Christ raised:

And if Christ be not raised, your faith *is* vain; ye are yet in your sins.

Then they also which are fallen asleep in Christ are perished *(like the dog; or unbelieving?)*.

If in this life only we have hope in Christ *(, there is no hope of the next life)*, we are of all men most miserable *(and all is vain as Solomon explained)*.

1 Corinthians 15:12 through 15:19

Our only labor required for eternal reward is that we walk in faith of Jesus resurrected from the dead for our deliverance unto life everlasting; John 3:16!

But now is Christ risen from the dead, *and* become the firstfruits *(of the Fathers harvest; and first born from the dead)* of them that slept *(die in faith of Him)*.

For since by man *(Adam)* came death, by man *(Jesus)* came also the resurrection of the dead.

For as in Adam all die, *(but then)* even so in Christ *(Jesus)* shall all be made alive *(unto eternal life, <u>if they believe</u>)*.

But every man in his own order *(of living, believing, and then death)*: Christ *(Jesus)* the firstfruits *(of the Fathers harvest; and first born from the dead)*; afterward they that are Christ's *(or belong to Christ)* at his *second (2nd)* coming.

Then *cometh* the end *(as we have known in sinful flesh)*, when he *(Jesus)* shall have delivered up the kingdom to God, even the Father; when he *(Jesus)* shall have put down all *(other)* rule and all *(other)* authority and power *(including the power and authority of death)*.

For he *(Jesus)* must reign, till he hath put all enemies under his feet.

The last enemy *that* shall be destroyed *is* death.

For he *(Jesus)* hath put all things under his feet *(or, triumphed over them things)*. But when he saith all things are put under *him, it is* manifest that he is excepted *(or accepted\ approved of God the Father)*, which did put all things under him *(Jesus)*.

And when all things shall be subdued unto him *(Jesus)*, then shall the Son *(Jesus)* also himself be subject unto him *(God the Father)* that put all things under him *(Jesus, the Son)*, that God *(or, the God Head)* may be all in all.

Else *(or otherwise)* what shall they *(that believe)* do which are baptized for the dead, if the dead rise not at all? why are they then baptized for the dead?

And why stand we in jeopardy *(of death)* every hour?

I protest *(against death)* by *(or through)* your rejoicing which I have in Christ Jesus our Lord, *(because)* I die daily.

If after the manner of men I have fought with beasts *(those that <u>would not believe</u> according to the Gospel of Jesus)* at Ephesus, what advantageth it me, if the dead rise not? *(Then)*, let us eat and drink; for to morrow we die *(is all that anyone has to look forward to)*.

Be not deceived: evil *(and/ or wrong)* communications corrupt good manners *(or in this case, "hope of better days to come")*.

Awake to righteousness, and sin not; for some have not the knowledge of God: I speak *this* to your shame *(that do not **believe** God).*
1 Corinthians 15:20 through 15:34

Paul the apostle describes resurrection for those that believes the resurrection of Jesus for deliverance, salvation, forgiveness of sin unto eternal life.

But some *(doubting and unbelieving)* will say, How are the dead raised up? and with what body do they come?
Thou fool, that which thou sowest is not quickened *(made alive and new)*, except it die:
And that which thou sowest, thou sowest not that body that shall be, but bare grain *(being swooned, old)*, it may chance *(or may be)* of wheat, or of some other *(grain, but the principle is the same)*
But God giveth it a body as it hath pleased him, and to every seed his own body.
All flesh *is* not the same flesh: but *there is* one *kind of* flesh of men, another flesh of beasts, another of fishes, *and* another of birds.
There are also celestial *(or heavenly)* bodies, and bodies terrestrial *(earthy)*: but the glory of the celestial *(heavenly) is* one, and the *glory* of the terrestrial *(earthy) is* another.
There is one glory *(beauty/ magnificence/ brilliance)* of the sun, and another glory of the moon, and another glory of the stars: for *one* star differeth from *another* star in glory *(or brilliance)*.
So also *is* the resurrection of the dead. It is sown in corruption; it is raised in incorruption:
It is sown in dishonour; it is raised in glory: it is sown in weakness; it is raised in power:
It is sown a natural body *(or old grain)*; it is raised a spiritual body *(eternal glory)*. There is a natural body, and there is a spiritual body.
And so it is written, The first *(1st)* man Adam was made a living soul; the last Adam *(Jesus) was made* a quickening spirit *(or, given spiritual life eternally)*.
Howbeit that *was* not first *(1st)* which is spiritual, but that which is natural *(carnal)*; and afterward that which is spiritual.

The first *(1ˢᵗ)* man *(Adam)* is of the earth, earthy: the second *(2ⁿᵈ)* man *is* the Lord *(Jesus)* from heaven.

As *is* the earthy, such *are* they also that are earthy *(terrestrial or old grain)*: and as *is* the heavenly, such *are* they also that are heavenly *(resurrected with spiritual life eternally)*.

And as we *(that believe)* have borne the image of the earthy, we shall also bear the image of the heavenly.

Now this I say, brethren, that flesh and blood *(carnal or earthy)* cannot inherit the kingdom of God; neither doth corruption inherit incorruption.

Behold, I shew you a mystery; We shall not all sleep *(as to be dead in graves?)*, but we shall all be changed *(which believe)*,

In a moment, in the twinkling of an eye, at the last trump: for the trumpet shall sound, and the dead *(or those died in the past, believing for eternal life through Christ Jesus)* shall be raised incorruptible, and we *(that are naturally alive/ breathing at that moment)* shall be changed *(if we believe for resurrection in Christ Jesus)*.

For this corruptible must put on incorruption, and this mortal *must* put on immortality.

So when this corruptible shall have put on incorruption, and this mortal shall have put on immortality, then shall be brought to pass the saying that is written, Death is swallowed up in victory *(Isaiah 25:8)*.

O death, where *is* thy sting? O grave, where *is* thy victory?

The sting of death *is* sin; and the strength of sin *is* the law *(because of the weakness of the flesh to accomplish the law) (Romans 8:3)*.

But thanks *be* to God, which giveth us the victory through our Lord Jesus Christ *(; the victory that is required of us according to law, which we could not achieve, except in Christ Jesus)*.

Therefore, my beloved brethren, be ye stedfast, unmoveable, always abounding in the work of *(faith in)* the Lord (Jesus Christ), forasmuch as ye know that your labour *(of faith)* is not in vain in the Lord *(Jesus Christ)*.

1 Corinthians 15:35 through 15:58

And so vanity, as declared by Solomon shall only result when an individual go to the grave having rejected, and\ or not truly received the gift of salvation in Christ Jesus, according to John 3:16:

And as Moses lifted up the serpent in the wilderness, even so must the Son of man be lifted up:

That whosoever **believeth** in him should not perish, but have eternal life.

Joh 3:16 For God so loved the world, that he gave his only begotten Son, that whosoever **believeth** in him should not perish, but have everlasting life.

For God sent not his Son into the world to condemn the world; but that the world through him might be saved.

He that **believeth** on him is not condemned: but he that **believeth not** is condemned already, because he hath not **believed** in the name of the only begotten Son of God.

And this is the condemnation, that light is come into the world, and men loved darkness rather than light, because their deeds were evil.

For every one that doeth evil hateth the light, neither cometh to the light, lest his deeds should be reproved.

But he that doeth truth cometh to the light, that his deeds may be made manifest, that they are wrought in God.

John 3:14 through 3:21

Ecclesiastes Chapter 4

What Help is There for the Oppressed Without A Comforter

Ecc 4:1 So I returned, and considered all the oppressions that are done under the sun: and behold the tears of *such as were* oppressed, and they had no comforter; and on the side of their oppressors *there was* power; but they had no comforter.

Ecc 4:2 Wherefore I praised the dead which are already dead more than the living which are yet alive.

Ecc 4:3 Yea, better *is he (the dead)* than both they, which hath not yet been, who hath not seen the evil work that is done under the sun.

Ecc 4:4 Again, I considered all travail, and every right work, that for this a man is envied of his neighbour. This *is* also vanity and vexation of spirit.

Ecc 4:5 The fool foldeth his hands together *(doing nothing?)*, and eateth his own flesh *(or die of starvation?)*.

Ecc 4:6 Better *is* an handful *with* quietness, than both the hands full *with* travail and vexation of spirit.

Ecc 4:7 Then I returned, and I saw vanity under the sun.

Ecc 4:8 There is one *alone,* and *there is* not a second *(companion, or relative?)*; yea, he hath neither child nor brother: yet *is there* no end of all his labour; neither is his eye satisfied with riches; neither *saith he,* For whom do I labour, and bereave my soul of good *(or leave my goods to when I die)*? This *is* also vanity, yea, it *is* a sore *(or agonizing)* travail.

Ecc 4:9 Two *(2) are* better than one *(1)*; because they have a good *(or greater)* reward *(gain)* for their labour.

Ecc 4:10 For if they fall, the one will lift up his fellow: but woe to him *that is* alone when he falleth; for *he hath* not another to help him up.

Ecc 4:11 Again, if two *(2)* lie together, then they have heat: but how can one *(1)* be warm *alone?*

Ecc 4:12 And if one *(1)* prevail against him, two *(2)* shall withstand him *(the one)*; and a threefold cord is not quickly broken *(because it is stronger than a single fold cord)*.

Ecc 4:13 Better *is* a poor and a wise child than an old and foolish king, who will no more be admonished *(or corrected because he is king?)*.

Ecc 4:14 For out of prison he cometh to reign; whereas also *he that is* born in his kingdom becometh poor.

Ecc 4:15 I considered all the living which walk under the sun, with the second child that shall stand up in his stead.

Ecc 4:16 *There is* no end of all the people, *even* of all that have been before them: they also that come after shall not rejoice in him. Surely this also *is* vanity and vexation of spirit.

Ecclesiastes Chapter 5

Being Mindful of Right Behavior before the LORD God

Ecc 5:1 Keep thy foot *(or know thy place?)* when thou goest to the house of God, and be more ready to hear, than to give the sacrifice of fools *(which is poor instructions, or council?)*: for they *(fools)* consider not that they do evil.

Ecc 5:2 Be not rash *(or lack of careful consideration)* with thy mouth, and let not thine heart be hasty to utter any thing before God: for God *is* in heaven, and thou upon earth: therefore let thy words be few.

Ecc 5:3 For a dream cometh through the multitude of business; and a fool's voice *is known* by multitude of words.

Ecc 5:4 When thou vowest a vow unto God, defer not to pay it; for *he hath* no pleasure in fools: pay that which thou hast vowed.

Ecc 5:5 Better *is it* that thou shouldest not vow, than that thou shouldest vow and not pay.

Ecc 5:6 Suffer not thy mouth to cause thy flesh to sin; neither say thou before the angel, that it *was* an error: wherefore *(or why)* should God be angry at thy voice, and destroy the work of thine hands?

Ecc 5:7 For in the multitude of dreams and many words *there are* also *divers* vanities: but fear thou God.

Ecc 5:8 If thou seest the oppression of the poor, and violent perverting of judgment and justice in a province, marvel not at the matter: for *he that is* higher than the highest regardeth; and *there be* higher than they.

Ecc 5:9 Moreover the profit of the earth is for all: the king *himself* is served by the field.

Ecc 5:10 He that loveth silver shall not be satisfied with silver; nor he that loveth abundance with increase: this *is* also vanity.

Ecc 5:11 When goods increase, they are increased that eat them: and what good *is there* to the owners thereof, saving the beholding *of them* with their eyes?

Ecc 5:12 The sleep of a labouring man *is* sweet, whether he eat little or much: but the abundance of the rich will not suffer him to sleep *(when he worry about how to keep his riches?)*.

Ecc 5:13 There is a sore *(or agonizing)* evil *which* I have seen under the sun, *namely*, riches kept for the owners thereof to their hurt.

Ecc 5:14 But those riches perish by evil travail *(or struggle)*: and he begetteth a son, and *there is* nothing in his hand.

Ecc 5:15 As he came forth of his mother's womb, naked shall he return to go as he came, and shall take nothing of his labour, which he may carry away in his hand.

Ecc 5:16 And this also *is* a sore *(or agonizing)* evil, *that* in all points as he came, so shall he go: and what profit hath he that hath laboured for the wind?

Ecc 5:17 All his days also he eateth in darkness, and *he hath* much sorrow and wrath with his sickness.

Ecc 5:18 Behold *that* which I have seen: *it is* good and comely *for one* to eat and to drink, and to enjoy the good of all his labour that he taketh under the sun all the days of his life, which God giveth him: for it *is* his portion.

Ecc 5:19 Every man also to whom God hath given riches and wealth, and hath given him power to eat thereof, and to take his portion, and to rejoice in his labour; this *is* the gift of God.

Ecc 5:20 For he shall not much remember *(or regret?)* the days of his life; because God answereth *him* in the joy of his heart.

Ecclesiastes Chapter 6

Everyone Seeks to Enjoy the Gains from Their Labor

Ecc 6:1 There is an evil which I have seen under the sun, and it *is* common among men:

Ecc 6:2 A man to whom God hath given riches, wealth, and honour, so that he wanteth nothing for his soul of all that he desireth, yet

God giveth him not power to eat thereof, but a stranger eateth it: this *is* vanity, and it *is* an evil disease.

Ecc 6:3 If a man beget an hundred *(100) children,* and live many years, so that the days of his years be many, and his soul be not filled with good *(to do good?),* and also *that* he have no burial *(live many years?);* I say, *that* an untimely birth *is* better than he.

Ecc 6:4 For he *(of untimely birth?)* cometh in with vanity, and departeth in darkness, and his name shall be covered with darkness.

Ecc 6:5 Moreover *(if?)* he *(of untimely birth?)* hath not seen the sun *(or lived a very short while?),* nor known *any thing:* this hath more rest than the other *(of no burial or lived many years?).*

Ecc 6:6 Yea, though he live a thousand *(1000)* years twice *told,* yet hath he seen no good: do not all go to one place?

Ecc 6:7 All the labour of man *is* for his mouth *(or food),* and yet the appetite is not filled.

Ecc 6:8 For what hath the wise more than the fool? what hath the poor, that knoweth to walk before the living?

Ecc 6:9 Better *is* the sight of the eyes than the wandering of the desire: this *is* also vanity and vexation of spirit.

Ecc 6:10 That which hath been is named *(or identified)* already, and it is known that it *is* man: neither may he contend with him that is mightier than he.

Ecc 6:11 Seeing there be many things that increase vanity, what *is* man the better?

Ecc 6:12 For who knoweth what *is* good for man in *this* life, all the days of his vain life which he spendeth as a shadow *(or very short while)?* for who can tell a man what shall be after him under the sun *(the answer to this was not fully reveal until the ministry of Jesus, by Jesus; "though some may consider it an unbelievable, or unrealistic answer", Paul the Apostle talks about it in our commentary provided after Ecclesiastes Chapter 3 verse 22 above)?*

Ecclesiastes Chapter 7

There are Obstacles to Gaining a Good Reputation

Ecc 7:1 A good name *is* better than precious ointment; and the day of death than the day of one's birth.

Ecc 7:2 *It is* better to go to the house of mourning, than to go to the house of feasting: for that *is* the end of all men; and the living will lay *it* to his heart.

Ecc 7:3 Sorrow *is* better than laughter: for by the sadness of the countenance the heart is made better.

Ecc 7:4 The heart of the wise *is* in the house of mourning; but the heart of fools *is* in the house of mirth *(or merriment)*.

Ecc 7:5 *It is* better to hear the rebuke of the wise, than for a man to hear the song of fools.

Ecc 7:6 For as the crackling of thorns under a pot, so *is* the laughter of the fool: this also *is* vanity.

Ecc 7:7 Surely oppression maketh a wise man mad; and a gift destroyeth the heart.

Ecc 7:8 Better *is* the end of a thing than the beginning thereof: *and* the patient in spirit *is* better than the proud in spirit.

Ecc 7:9 Be not hasty in thy spirit to be angry: for anger resteth in the bosom of fools.

Ecc 7:10 Say not thou, What is *the cause* that the former days were better than these? for thou dost not enquire wisely concerning this.

Ecc 7:11 Wisdom *is* good with an inheritance: and *by it there is* profit to them that see the sun.

Ecc 7:12 For wisdom *is* a defence, *and* money *is* a defence: but the excellency of knowledge *is, that* wisdom giveth life to them that have it.

Ecc 7:13 Consider the work of God: for who can make *that* straight, which he hath made crooked?

Ecc 7:14 In the day of prosperity be joyful, but in the day of adversity consider: God also hath set the one *(the day of prosperity)* over against the other *(the day of adversity)*, to the end that man should find nothing after him *(the answer to this was not fully reveal until the ministry of Jesus, by Jesus; "though some may consider it an unbelievable, or unrealistic answer", Paul the Apostle talks about it in our commentary provided after Ecclesiastes Chapter 3 verse 22 above).*

Ecc 7:15 All *things* have I seen in the days of my vanity: there is a just *man* that perisheth in his righteousness, and there is a wicked *man* that prolongeth *his life* in his wickedness.

Ecc 7:16 Be not righteous over much; neither make thyself over wise: why shouldest thou destroy thyself?

Ecc 7:17 Be not over much wicked, neither be thou foolish: why shouldest thou die before thy time?

Ecc 7:18 *It is* good that thou shouldest take hold of this; yea, also from this withdraw not thine hand: for he that feareth God shall come forth of them all.

Ecc 7:19 Wisdom strengtheneth the wise more than ten *(10)* mighty *men* which are in the city.

Ecc 7:20 For *there is* not a just man upon earth, that doeth good, and sinneth not.

Ecc 7:21 Also take no heed unto all words that are spoken; lest thou hear thy servant curse thee:

Ecc 7:22 For oftentimes also thine own heart knoweth that thou thyself likewise hast cursed others.

Ecc 7:23 All this have I proved by wisdom: I said, I will be wise; but it *was* far from me.

Ecc 7:24 That which is far off, and exceeding deep, who can find it out?

Ecc 7:25 I applied mine heart to know, and to search, and to seek out wisdom, and the reason *of things,* and to know the wickedness of folly, even of foolishness *and* madness:

Ecc 7:26 And I find more bitter than death the woman, whose heart *is* snares and nets, *and* her hands *as* bands: whoso pleaseth God shall escape from her; but the sinner shall be taken by her.

Ecc 7:27 Behold, this have I found, saith the preacher, *counting* one by one, to find out the account:

Ecc 7:28 Which yet my soul seeketh, but I find not: one man among a thousand *(1000)* have I found; but a woman among all those have I not found.

Ecc 7:29 Lo, this only have I found, that God hath made man upright; but they have sought out many inventions *(or ways that exclude the LORD God?)*.

Ecclesiastes Chapter 8

Ecc 8:1 Who *is* as the wise *man?* and who knoweth the interpretation of a thing? a man's wisdom maketh his face to shine, and the boldness of his face shall be changed.

Ecc 8:2 I *counsel thee* to keep the king's commandment, and *that* in regard of the oath of God.

Ecc 8:3 Be not hasty to go out of his sight: stand not in an evil thing; for he doeth whatsoever pleaseth him.

Ecc 8:4 Where the word of a king *is, there is* power: and who may say unto him, What doest thou?

Ecc 8:5 Whoso keepeth the commandment shall feel no evil thing: and a wise man's heart discerneth both time and judgment.

Ecc 8:6 Because to every purpose there is time and judgment, therefore the misery of man *is* great upon him.

Ecc 8:7 For he knoweth not that which shall be: for who can tell him when it shall be?

Ecc 8:8 *There is* no man that hath power over the spirit to retain the spirit; neither *hath he* power in the day of death: and *there is* no discharge in *that* war; neither shall wickedness deliver those that are given to it.

Ecc 8:9 All this have I seen, and applied my heart unto every work that is done under the sun: *there is* a time wherein one man ruleth over another to his own hurt.

Ecc 8:10 And so I saw the wicked buried, who had come and gone from the place of the holy, and they were forgotten in the city where they had so done: this *is* also vanity.

Ecc 8:11 Because sentence against an evil work is not executed speedily, therefore the heart of the sons of men is fully set in them to do evil.

Ecc 8:12 Though a sinner do evil an hundred *(100)* times, and his *days* be prolonged, yet surely I know that it shall be well with them that fear God, which fear before him:

Ecc 8:13 But it shall not be well with the wicked, neither shall he prolong *his* days, *which are* as a shadow; because he feareth not before God.

Ecc 8:14 There is a vanity which is done upon the earth; that there be just *men,* unto whom it happeneth according to the work of the wicked; again, there be wicked *men,* to whom it happeneth according to the work of the righteous: I said that this also *is* vanity.

Ecc 8:15 Then I commended mirth *(merriment)*, because a man hath no better thing under the sun, than to eat, and to drink, and to be merry: for that shall abide with him of his labour the days of his life, which God giveth him under the sun.

Ecc 8:16 When I applied mine heart to know wisdom, and to see the business that is done upon the earth: (for also *there is that* neither day nor night seeth sleep with his eyes:)

Ecc 8:17 Then I beheld all the work of God, that a man cannot find out the work that is done under the sun: because though a man labour to seek *it* out, yet he shall not find *it;* yea further; though a wise *man* think to know *it,* yet shall he not be able to find *it.*

Ecclesiastes Chapter 9

The LORD God Has Subjected All to the Same "Whosoever Requirements"

Ecc 9:1 For all this I considered in my heart even to declare all this, that the righteous, and the wise, and their works, *are* in the hand of God: no man knoweth either love or hatred *by* all *that is* before them.

Ecc 9:2 All *things come* alike to all: *there is* one event to the righteous, and to the wicked; to the good and to the clean, and to the unclean; to him that sacrificeth, and to him that sacrificeth not: as *is* the good, so *is* the sinner; *and* he that sweareth, as *he* that feareth an oath.

Ecc 9:3 This *is* an evil among all *things* that are done under the sun, that *there is* one event unto all: yea, also the heart of the sons of men is full of evil, and madness *is* in their heart while they live, and after that *they go* to the dead.

Ecc 9:4 For to him that is joined to all the living there is hope: for a living dog is better than a dead lion *(or a living dog is more fearsome than a dead lion?)*.

Ecc 9:5 For the living know that they shall die: but the dead know not any thing, neither have they any more a reward; for the memory of them is forgotten.

Ecc 9:6 Also their love, and their hatred, and their envy, is now perished; neither have they any more a portion for ever in any *thing* that is done under the sun.

Ecc 9:7 Go thy way, eat thy bread with joy, and drink thy wine with a merry heart; for God now accepteth thy works.

Ecc 9:8 Let thy garments be always white; and let thy head lack no ointment.

Ecc 9:9 Live joyfully with the wife whom thou lovest all the days of the life of thy vanity, which he hath given thee under the sun, all the days of thy vanity: for that *is* thy portion in *this* life, and in thy labour which thou takest under the sun.

Ecc 9:10 Whatsoever thy hand findeth to do, do *it* with thy might; for *there is* no work, nor device, nor knowledge, nor wisdom, in the grave, whither thou goest.

Ecc 9:11 I returned, and saw under the sun, that the race *is* not to the swift, nor the battle to the strong, neither yet bread to the wise, nor yet riches to men of understanding, nor yet favour to men of skill; but time and chance happeneth to them all.

Ecc 9:12 For man also knoweth not his time: as the fishes that are taken in an evil net, and as the birds that are caught in the snare; so *are* the sons of men snared in an evil time, when it falleth suddenly upon them.

Ecc 9:13 This wisdom have I seen also under the sun, and it *seemed* great unto me:

Ecc 9:14 *There was* a little city, and few men within it; and there came a great king against it, and besieged it, and built great bulwarks against it:

Ecc 9:15 Now there was found in it a poor wise man, and he by his wisdom delivered the city; yet no man remembered that same poor man.

Ecc 9:16 Then said I, Wisdom *is* better than strength: nevertheless the poor man's wisdom *is* despised, and his words are not heard.

Ecc 9:17 The words of wise *men are* heard in quiet more than the cry of him that ruleth among fools.

Ecc 9:18 Wisdom *is* better than weapons of war: but one sinner destroyeth much good.

Ecclesiastes Chapter 10

Ecc 10:1 Dead flies cause the ointment of the apothecary *(or pharmacy)* to send forth a stinking savour: *so doth* a little folly him that is in reputation *(or known)* for wisdom *and* honour.

Ecc 10:2 A wise man's heart *is* at his right hand; but a fool's heart at his left.

Ecc 10:3 Yea also, when he that is a fool walketh by the way, his wisdom faileth *him*, and he saith to every one *that* he *is* a fool.

Ecc 10:4 If the spirit of the ruler rise up against thee, leave not thy place; for yielding pacifieth great offences *(in other words, "stand your ground")*.

Ecc 10:5 There is an evil *which* I have seen under the sun, as an error *which* proceedeth from the ruler:

Ecc 10:6 Folly is set in great dignity, and the rich sit in low place.

Ecc 10:7 I have seen servants upon horses, and princes walking as servants upon the earth.

Ecc 10:8 He that diggeth a pit shall fall into it; and whoso breaketh an hedge, a serpent shall bite him.

Ecc 10:9 Whoso removeth stones shall be hurt therewith; *and* he that cleaveth wood shall be endangered thereby.

Ecc 10:10 If the iron *(or cutting tool?)* be blunt *(or dull?)*, and he do not whet *(or sharpen?)* the edge, then must he put to more strength: but wisdom *is* profitable to direct.

Ecc 10:11 Surely the serpent will bite without enchantment; and a babbler is no better.

Ecc 10:12 The words of a wise man's mouth *are* gracious; but the lips of a fool will swallow up himself.

Ecc 10:13 The beginning of the words of his mouth *is* foolishness: and the end of his talk *is* mischievous madness.

Ecc 10:14 A fool also is full of words: a man cannot tell what shall be; and what shall be after him, who can tell him *(the answer to this was not fully reveal until the ministry of Jesus, by Jesus; "though some may consider it an unbelievable, or unrealistic answer", Paul the Apostle talks about it in our commentary provided after Ecclesiastes Chapter 3 verse 22 above)*?

Ecc 10:15 The labour of the foolish wearieth every one of them, because he knoweth not how to go to the city.

Ecc 10:16 Woe to thee, O land, when thy king *is* a child, and thy princes eat in the morning!

Ecc 10:17 Blessed *art* thou, O land, when thy king *is* the son of nobles, and thy princes eat in due season, for strength, and not for drunkenness!

Ecc 10:18 By much slothfulness the building decayeth; and through idleness of the hands the house droppeth through.

Ecc 10:19 A feast is made for laughter, and wine maketh merry: but money answereth all *things*.

Ecc 10:20 Curse not the king, no not in thy thought; and curse not the rich in thy bedchamber: for a bird of the air shall carry the voice, and that which hath wings shall tell the matter.

Ecclesiastes Chapter 11

Ecc 11:1 Cast thy bread upon the waters: for thou shalt find it after many days.

Ecc 11:2 Give a portion to seven *(7)*, and also to eight *(8) (this generate personal favors, and help others?)*; for thou knowest not what evil shall be upon the earth.

Ecc 11:3 If the clouds be full of rain, they empty *themselves* upon the earth: and if the tree fall toward the south, or toward the north, in the place where the tree falleth, there it shall be.

Ecc 11:4 He that observeth the wind shall not sow; and he that regardeth the clouds shall not reap *(Waiting for the right condition to act can sometimes be counter productive?)*.

Ecc 11:5 As thou knowest not what *is* the way of the spirit *(Holy Spirit of God, nor* how the bones *do grow* in the womb of her that is with child: even so thou knowest not the works of God who maketh all.

Ecc 11:6 In the morning sow thy seed, and in the evening withhold not thine hand *(from being generous?)*: for thou knowest not whether shall prosper, either this or that, or whether they both *shall be* alike good.

Ecc 11:7 Truly the light *is* sweet, and a pleasant *thing it is* for the eyes to behold the sun:

Ecc 11:8 But if a man live many years, *and* rejoice in them all; yet let him remember the days of darkness; for they shall be many. All that cometh *is* vanity.

Ecc 11:9 Rejoice, O young man, in thy youth; and let thy heart cheer thee in the days of thy youth, and walk in the ways of thine heart, and in the sight of thine eyes: but know thou, that for all these *things* God will bring thee into judgment.

Ecc 11:10 Therefore remove sorrow from thy heart, and put away evil from thy flesh: for childhood and youth *are* vanity.

Ecclesiastes Chapter 12

Ecc 12:1 Remember now thy Creator in the days of thy youth, while the evil days come not, nor the years draw nigh *(or old age)*, when thou shalt say, I have no pleasure in them *(no longer youthful days?)*;

Ecc 12:2 While the sun, or the light, or the moon, or the stars, be not darkened, nor the clouds return after the rain *(or time of death)*:

Ecc 12:3 In the day when the keepers *(or hands?)* of the house *(body?)* shall tremble, and the strong men *(legs?)* shall bow themselves, and the grinders *(teeth)* cease because they are few, and those that look out of the windows *(the eyes)* be darkened,

Ecc 12:4 And the doors shall be shut in the streets, when the sound of the grinding is low *(or there is loss of hearing)*, and he shall rise up at the voice of the bird *(not requiring much sleep)*, and all the daughters of musick shall be brought low *(there is less and less activity; one become less adventurous; fright, agitation, and confusion increases because of increased age!)*;

Ecc 12:5 Also *when* they shall be afraid of *that which is* high, and fears *shall be* in the way, and the almond tree shall flourish *(or can not see past blurring eyesight?)*, and the grasshopper shall be a burden *(or little noises are upsetting?)*, and desire shall fail: because man goeth to his long home, and the mourners go about the streets:

Ecc 12:6 Or ever the silver cord be loosed, or the golden bowl be broken, or the pitcher be broken at the fountain, or the wheel broken at the cistern *(thus, connection(s) to this life be severed!)*.

Ecc 12:7 Then shall the dust *(or natural body)* return to the earth as it was: and the spirit shall return unto God who gave it *(Refer to, "The Kinsman Redeemer" in the "Definition & Figures" section)*.

Ecc 12:8 Vanity of vanities, saith the preacher; all *is* vanity *(the possibility for this not resulting in an individual's final disposition of existence was not fully reveal until the ministry of Jesus, by Jesus; "though some may consider it an unbelievable, or unrealistic answer", Paul the Apostle talks about it in our commentary provided after Ecclesiastes Chapter 3 verse 22 above)*.

Ecc 12:9 And moreover, because the preacher was wise, he still taught the people knowledge; yea, he gave good heed, and sought out, *and* set in order many proverbs.

Ecc 12:10 The preacher sought to find out acceptable words: and *that which was* written *was* upright, *even* words of truth.

Ecc 12:11 The words of the wise *are* as goads, and as nails fastened *by* the masters of assemblies, *which* are given from one shepherd.

Ecc 12:12 And further, by these, my son, be admonished: of making many books *there is* no end; and much study *is* a weariness of the flesh.

Ecc 12:13 Let us hear the conclusion of the whole matter: Fear God, and keep his commandments: for this *is* the whole *duty* of man.

Ecc 12:14 For God shall bring every work into judgment, with every secret thing, whether *it be* good, or whether *it be* evil ***(this verse speaks of the time of regeneration, or resurrection)***.

==============================

A Summary of Ecclesiastes

I am persuaded King Solomon sets a witness in place, which all may see as example of how things are according to natural forces; and absent of salvation's revelation, according to the Gospel of Jesus, that is summed up in ***John 3:16!***

Therefore, after Adam, and before the "manifested revealing" of Jesus, the lives of men, and even the natural forces displays prescribed patterns of repetitions; which Solomon saw as, "vanity"; "vanity of vanities, all is vanity", Solomon said! And the best that anyone could hope for ***(because of vanity)*** is to enjoy the fruit of one's labor while the time is now, because the days described in ***Ecclesiastes Chapter 12*** comes upon all who ever lives. Thus, the body returns to dust just as that of the dog; and "seemingly", the human spirit goes to God where it remains dormant! But how long ….. ; Forever?

Read again *Ecclesiastes Chapter 3*, followed by our imbedded commentary, as we put forth efforts to explain the answer(s) God provided through His Son, the *Lord Jesus Christ; whereby vanity is defeated*!

Today, we are given to know *through the teachings of Jesus our Savior*, the final Chapters of the disposition that the LORD God has made available for human life and living, when we believe *the teachings of Jesus our Savior*!

Our explanations of answers from God continue after *Ecclesiastes Chapter 3*, as follows:

Where God is, vanity has no place, nor ability!

- God our Creator has brought the human race to an awesome **opportunity** for decision, which is, "life eternal as He is; or else oblivion as the dog and hellfire shall be the only option that remains for the individual"!
- But the majority of earth's population; like dumb animals grazing unawares, have not recognized the **opportunity**!
- Many of the majority is so busy with other things of creation, they refuse to believe He *(the LORD God) is responsible for bringing forth* the other things of creation, or them!
- Many of the majority is so much in awe of things made, and the heavens, which *the LORD God* put in place, they choose not to believe He could have possibly been the author; but they believe everything came of spontaneous origin (i.e., the "Big Bang")!
- Therefore, they accept that the Universe is eternal, but an eternal one could not have possibly created it! And only *the Eternal LORD God* knows how much an individual's faith chases after such imaginations as these "Big Bang Theories"!
- Many of the majority is so busy living this present short "breath of life" that they have not taken time out to think about the possibilities of promises concerning the next, "regenerated, born-again life"

according to John 3:16: Which is the life promised of God through *the Sacrifice of Jesus Christ; the Message of the Cross!*

Many of the majority has already swallowed such abundance of lies and deception that they will not, or can not be convinced of what is true; which is **the LORD God** of Creation is "God" **and Jesus is His Son**!

And so, **the Lord Jesus** cautions His <u>**followers and believers**</u> as provided below:

Mat 7:1 Judge not, that ye be not judged *(or punishment\ destruction for anyone is not ours to decide! But we must discern the evil, that we may only embrace the good; the right, and reject evil!)*.

Mat 7:2 For with what judgment ye judge, ye shall be judged: and with what measure ye mete, it shall be measured to you again.

Mat 7:3 And why beholdest thou the mote *(speck)* that is in thy brother's eye, but considerest not the beam *(telephone pole)* that is in thine own eye?

Mat 7:4 Or how wilt thou say to thy brother, Let me pull out the mote *(speck)* out of thine eye; and, behold, a beam *(telephone pole)* is in thine own eye?

Mat 7:5 Thou hypocrite, first cast out the beam *(telephone pole)* out of thine own eye; and then shalt thou see clearly to cast out the mote *(speck)* out of thy brother's eye.

Mat 7:6 Give not that which is holy unto the dogs, neither cast ye your pearls before swine, lest they *(dogs and swine)* trample them *(your pearls)* under their feet, and turn again and rend *(or rip)* you *(think of what Jesus said this way: When you witness to someone, and they are doggedly determined to reject the Gospel, shake the dust off your feet for a testimony against them! (See Mathew 10:14; Mark 6:11; Luke 9:5)*.

Mat 7:7 Ask, and it shall be given you; seek, and ye shall find; knock, and it shall be opened unto you:

Mat 7:8 For every one that asketh receiveth; and he that seeketh findeth; and to him that knocketh it shall be opened.

Mat 7:9 Or what man is there of you, whom if his son ask bread, will he give him a stone?

Mat 7:10 Or if he ask a fish, will he give him a serpent?

Mat 7:11 If ye then, being evil, know how to give good gifts unto your children, how much more shall your Father which is in heaven give good things to them that ask him?

Mat 7:12 Therefore all things whatsoever ye would that men should do to you, do ye even so to them: for this is the law and the prophets *(or the law and the prophets instructs this)*.

Mat 7:13 Enter ye in at the strait gate: for wide *is* the gate, and broad *is* the way, that leadeth to destruction, and many there be which go in thereat:

Mat 7:14 Because strait *is* the gate, and narrow *is* the way, which leadeth unto life, and few there be that find it.

But ...

Joh 14:1 Let not your heart be troubled: ye believe in God, believe also in me.

Joh 14:2 In my Father's house are many mansions: if *it were* not *so*, I would have told you. I go to prepare a place for you.

Joh 14:3 And if I go and prepare a place for you, I will come again, and receive you unto myself; that where I am, *there* ye may be also.

Joh 14:4 And whither I go ye know, and the way ye know.

Joh 14:5 Thomas saith unto him *(Jesus)*, Lord, we know not whither thou goest; and how can we know the way?

Joh 14:6 Jesus saith unto him, I am the way, the truth, and the life: no man cometh unto the Father, but by me.

BOOK SUMMARY

God Uses Whomsoever, According to His Purpose

Jesus, Son of the Living God; Second Person of the Trinity and God Head: came of his own free will, and was sent of God the Father, according to His purpose, to deliver the human race from sin and iniquity unto eternal life. God the Son, Jesus is agreed with God the Father and God the Holy Spirit to be sent, called, and used for the purpose of God.

But let's consider first those lesser "called and used" of God, then we will examine the timeline of events in Scripture that brings whomsoever will "believe and come" to victory, liberty (SALVATION) by the sacrifice of Christ Jesus on the cross.

All we need do is study Old Testament Scripture a little bit to realize that God <u>uses</u> whom ever He will for His purpose, and/ or service; He is gracious to whom ever He would be gracious; and He show mercy upon whom He would show mercy. But then there are also those God <u>called</u>, and once He called them, that calling was not rescinded even when they despised, embarrassed, or disgraced their calling. And in the Old Testament it usually seems an important indication of whether God has called an individual is the fact that He identifies whom he called from their youth, or even before they were born.

This Bible Analysis shall undertake the effort to look at the <u>called</u> of God and those God <u>used</u> in Scripture during the time of their life and living; but whether <u>called</u> and/or <u>used</u>, God impacted them MIGHTILY according to His great power and purpose.

No calculated attempt shall be made to explain why God chose to call in one case, while he might only used whomsoever in another case; such understanding is in the mind of God unless He wants us to know, and tells us. But we must concede the obvious, which is God always knew whom he would **_use_** just as he knew whom he would **_call_** long before their time of living their earthly life!

Some would argue this is "Predestination". Not so! But as I said before, the choices God makes are in the mind of God unless He wants us to know, and tells us. Mortal understanding always fall short when compared with that of God, and we should be very, very, very careful about applying mortal judgments to such things concerning, "how the eternal God makes His choices."

For example, our first thoughts may be that God chooses whomsoever he will from those that are currently born and living. But he is eternal God, therefore, is he limited or bound by mortal expectations and explanations?

And by the way, predestination as we mortals understand it nullifies John 3:16!

My dear friends the LORD God Almighty is not a man that He should lie; but He is the same yesterday, and today, and forever (Numbers 23:19; 1Samuel 15:29; Hebrews 13:8)

> For my thoughts *are* not your thoughts, neither *are* your ways my ways, saith the LORD.
> For *as* the heavens are higher than the earth, so are my ways higher than your ways, and my thoughts than your thoughts.
> Isaiah 55:8 and 55:9

> And he said *(to Moses)*, I will make all my goodness pass before thee, and I will proclaim the name of the LORD before thee *(or before you get to where I send you, I will ensure they know that you are come*

in my behalf); and will be gracious to whom I will be gracious, and will shew mercy on whom I will shew mercy.

Exodus 33:19

But this Bible student is persuaded that God called Abraham and Sarah, even though the scriptures tell us very little about their youth. However, I believe we can say that He chose to only <u>use</u> Lot, the Nephew of Abraham, in Lot's time of living.

In no way should this statement be taken to mean that Lot died without God. We mortals are not qualified to make such a judgment; only God. But in my mind, even to be used of God is not to be despised in any way, because countless numbers of those that were neither called nor used in Scripture were *not* singled out of God (that is, of course, according to our seeing or observation).

Again, in no way should this statement be taken to mean that all those not mentioned in Biblical Scripture died without God. We mortals are not qualified to make such a judgment, because we can not know the final breaths of another's life; only God knows and that person; according to their presence of mind. And again I must repeat: such things are in the mind of God, alone. Who is qualified to council Him? Romans Chapter 14 verse 4 makes the case with great clarity for the relationship between mortal servant and master. How much more true this relationship is concerning the eternal God, and True Master of all?

Who art thou that judgest another man's servant? to his own master he standeth or falleth. Yea, he shall be holden up: for God is able to make him stand.

Rome 14:4

Covenant Men of Israel are <u>Called</u> and <u>Used</u> of God

The Lord God called Moses and kept him safe in the Palace of Pharaoh. He instructed him by name and went with him as he led the chosen people, Israel. Thus, Moses was called and chosen, and the family that became the

Nation of Israel was chosen and called. That calling has not been rescinded even unto this present day, although they dishonored their calling on more than one occasion throughout the centuries:

> Now therefore, I pray thee, if I *(Moses)* have found grace in thy sight, shew me now thy way, that I may know thee, that I may find grace in thy sight: and consider *(unto knowing?)* that this nation *(Israel)* is thy people.
> And he *(the LORD God)* said, My presence shall go *with thee*, and I will give thee rest.
> And he *(Moses)* said unto him *(the LORD God)*, If thy presence go not *with me*, carry us not up hence *(out of Egypt into wilderness?)*.
>
> Exodus 33:13 through 33:15

==================================

The LORD God distinguishes Israel from all other people throughout world history:

> For wherein shall it be known here that I *(Moses)* and thy people *(Israel)* have found grace in thy sight *(O God)? Is it* not in that thou goest with us? So shall we be separated, I and thy people, from all the people that *are* upon the face of the earth.

==================================

Exodus 33:16

> And the LORD said unto Moses, I will do this thing also that thou hast spoken: for thou hast found grace in my sight, and I know thee by name.
> And he *(Moses)* said, I beseech thee, shew me thy glory.
> And he *(the LORD)* said, I will make all my goodness pass before thee, and I will proclaim the name of the LORD before thee *(or before you get to where I send you, I will ensure they know that you are come*

in my behalf); and will be gracious to whom I will be gracious, and will shew mercy on whom I will shew mercy.

And he *(the LORD)* said, *(But)* Thou canst not see my face: for there shall no man see me, and live.

And the LORD said, Behold, *there is* a place by me *(the Lord Jesus Christ?)*, and thou shalt stand upon a rock *(the Lord Jesus Christ?)*:

And it shall come to pass, while my glory passeth by, that I will put thee in a clift *(the split; wound; the opening)* of the rock *(of the Lord Jesus Christ?)*, and *(I, the LORD)* will cover thee with my hand while I pass by:

And I will take away mine hand, and thou shalt see my back parts: but my face shall not be seen.

Exodus 33:17 through 33:23

As Moses approached the time of his "earthly end of days", the LORD God instructs Moses to name Joshua his successor:

And Moses spake unto the LORD, saying,

Let the LORD, the God of the spirits of all flesh, set a man *(or leader)* over the congregation,

Which may go out before them, and which may go in before them, and which may lead them out, and which may bring them in; that the congregation of the LORD be not as sheep which have no shepherd.

And the LORD said unto Moses, Take thee Joshua the son of Nun, a man in whom *is* the spirit, and lay thine hand upon him;

And set him *(Joshua)* before Eleazar the priest, and before all the congregation; and give him *(Joshua)* a charge *(of leadership)* in their sight.

And thou *(Moses)* shalt put *some* of thine honour upon him *(Joshua)*, that all the congregation of the children of Israel may be obedient.

And he *(Joshua)* shall stand before Eleazar the priest, who shall ask counsel *(or instruction)* for him *(Joshua)* after the judgment of Urim *(refer to, "Urim and the Thummim" in the "Definitions & Figures" section)* before the LORD: at his *(Joshua's)* word shall they go out, and at his word they shall come in, *both* he, and all the children of Israel with him, even all the congregation.

And Moses did as the LORD commanded him: and he took Joshua, and set him before Eleazar the priest, and before all the congregation:

And he laid his hands upon him, and gave him a charge, as the LORD commanded by the hand of Moses.

Numbers 27:15 through 27:23

Old Testament Judges:

Of all the Judges in Old Testament Israel, I believe Samson (Judges Chapter 13) and Samuel (Samuel Chapter 1 and 3) were <u>called</u> of God. Scripture speaks of them from their youth; even before their conception. The others Judges were <u>used</u>, although mightily of God, at the time they were needed according to the purpose of God.

Now, it seems God did not call Saul of the tribe of Benjamin to be the first King of Israel. But it seems God only <u>used</u> Saul in that position until David from the tribe of Judah would become of age to fulfill this calling. We see that the Lord GOD discontinued using Saul as king over Israel in 1Samuel 15:22 and 15:23.

Remember we made the statement that we do not believe that God rescind a "calling". David despised his calling but he sincerely repented, and asked the Lord GOD forgiveness. God heard him, and brought him through his failure; but family tragedy did not depart from among the household of David ...

And Samuel said *(to Saul)*, Hath the LORD *as great* delight in burnt offerings and sacrifices, as in <u>obeying</u> the voice of the LORD? Behold, to obey *is* better than sacrifice, *and* to hearken than the fat of rams.

For rebellion *is as* the sin of witchcraft, and stubbornness *is as* iniquity and idolatry. Because thou *(Saul)* hast rejected the word *(or instruction)* of the LORD, he *(the LORD)* hath also rejected thee *(Saul)* from *being* king.

1Samuel 15:22 and 15:23

God said David despised his calling. But God chose to restore David, and did not rescind his calling:

And Nathan *(the prophet)* said to David, Thou *art* the man. Thus saith the LORD God of Israel, I anointed thee king over Israel, and I delivered thee out of the hand of Saul;
And I gave thee thy master's house, and thy master's wives into thy bosom, and gave thee the house *(or Nation)* of Israel and of Judah; and if *that had been* too little, I would moreover have given unto thee such and such things.
Wherefore hast thou despised the commandment of the LORD, to do evil in his sight? thou hast killed Uriah the Hittite with the sword, and hast taken his wife *to be* thy wife, and hast slain him with the sword of the children of Ammon.
Now therefore the sword shall never depart from thine house; because thou hast despised me, and hast taken the wife of Uriah the Hittite to be thy wife.
Thus saith the LORD, Behold, I will raise up evil against thee out of thine own house, and I will take thy wives before thine eyes, and give *them* unto thy neighbour, and he *(your enemy)* shall lie with thy wives in the sight of this sun.
For thou didst *it* secretly: but I will do this thing before all Israel, and before the sun.
And David said unto Nathan *(the prophet)*, I have sinned against the LORD. And Nathan said unto David, The LORD also hath put away thy sin; thou shalt not die.
Howbeit, because by this deed thou hast given great occasion to the enemies of the LORD to blaspheme, the child also *that is* born unto thee *(out of this sin)* shall surely die.

2Samuel 12:7 through 12:14

Now, I consider David's son Solomon only called in that God commanded David to declare him his successor, rather than one of his other sons.

But God was displeased with Solomon for the latter years of his reign over Israel, but He chose not to take the kingdom from Solomon because of his Father David.

God instructed Solomon not to bring gentile concubines and wives into Israel, but Solomon disobeyed God. As a result the influx of these gentiles brought their idol worship with them and caused Solomon and the people to sin against God, as the whole nation became idol worshippers. God said this was committing fornication against Him. Thus, Solomon caused the Nation of Israel to sin. God judged the whole nation for this in that He divided the nation unto destruction. And after the reign of Solomon all the tribes other than Judah, Benjamin, and Simeon were divided unto the Northern Kingdom: Samaria, and\ or Ephraim.

And the citizens among Judah with Simeon, and Benjamin were formed into the Southern Kingdom at Jerusalem.

In 722 B.C. God <u>used</u> the Nation of Assyria to execute judgment upon the Northern Kingdom, Samaria, and scatter the people. The Northern Kingdom of Israel never recovered!

Then in 586 B.C. God <u>used</u> Nebuchadnezzar King of Babylon to execute judgment/ destruction upon the Temple and City at Jerusalem (Judah of Israel, the Southern Kingdom). After 70 years of exile, God recovered Judah a "remnant" of Israel at Jerusalem (the Southern Kingdom).

Of course I am certain Assyria, nor Babylon, thought that they were being <u>used</u> of God. And their attitude was that of a "whomsoever" which insists that, "Only My Might Got Me Advantage". "It is only by my power that I am victorious"! And in that they were idol worshipers, I suspect they may have given their false gods some credit?

Jesus, the Sacrifice and Foundation for Every Other Sacrifice

The journeys of Moses, Joshua, and Israel after departing Egypt preceded the Prophet Zechariah by many years. But this prophecy of Zechariah helps to gain insight for offerings and sacrificing God commanded of the children of Israel.

This prophecy also reveals, in amazing symbolism, the description of events that would surround Jesus, Messiah as He finishes the sacrificial atoning work for salvation of the human race! Therefore, we consider it greatly beneficial to include this very important prophecy of *Zechariah Chapter 5*, in any study of the Judeo – Christian Bible Books!

The whole prophecy of Zechariah dates to the time of the rebuilding of the Temple at Jerusalem. The circumstance is that it had been, more or less, seventy *(70)* years since the temple and Jerusalem was destroyed by Nebuchadnezzar, king of Babylonians, around **586 B.C**. Also read the prophecies of *Jeremiah 25:11 through 25:12*, and *Jeremiah 29:10*.

Zechariah Chapter 1 verse 1 says it was currently the second *(2nd)* year of the reign of Darius, which is likely the same Darius spoken of in the Book of Daniel, the Books of Ezra, Haggai, and perhaps even Nehemiah.

The ordinances/ laws/ God commanded of the children of Israel by the hand of Moses pointed to the sin bearer for the human race; the Lord Jesus Christ, as described in this prophecy of Zechariah!

Zechariah Chapter 5

The LORD has judged the violation(s) of His commandments; and His commandments shall prevail without destroying the whole human race, but only because of the sacrifice of our Lord and Savior Jesus Christ!

This, Chapter 5 of Zechariah, prophesies the detail process concerning the one the LORD God of Creation has chosen to bear the weight of His broken Commandment(s)/ Law(s), such that He may forgive and deliver anyone that disobey, and brake His Law(s) which is, and\ or because of sin!

Thus, His love, mercy, and grace of forgiveness is made available to those guilty of his broken Law(s), through His special servant; sin bearer/ blood sacrifice/ Messiah/ Jesus, <u>alone</u>. Need I remind you of the scripture that says, "For <u>all</u> have sinned and come short of the glory of God"; Romans 3:23. Or Galatians 3:22, "But the scripture hath concluded <u>all</u> under sin, that the promise by faith of Jesus Christ might be given to them that believe".

But we of the household of God know the Lamb of God prevailed over death for the purpose of offering eternal life to the world, according to John 3:16:

Then I *(Zechariah)* turned, and lifted up mine eyes, and looked, and behold a flying roll *(upon which the commandments/ word/ judgments of the LORD are written?)*.
And he *(the angel that talked with me)* said unto me, What seest thou? And I *(Zechariah)* answered, I see a flying roll; the length thereof *is* twenty *(20)* cubits, and the breadth thereof ten *(10)* cubits *(or 30 feet by 15 feet)*.

Zechariah 5:1 and 5:2

The curse, and\ or condemnation of the broken Law(s) of God upon the race of man:

Then said he unto me, This *(broken Law(s))* is the curse that goeth forth over the face of the whole earth: for every one that stealeth shall be cut off *(die)* as on this side according to it *(the roll/ broken Law of God)*; and every one that sweareth shall be cut off *(die)* as on that side according to it *(the roll/ broken Law of God)*.
I *(the LORD)* will bring it *(my judgment/ curse/ broken law)* forth, saith the LORD of hosts, and it shall enter into the house of the thief *(and\ or the sinner)*, and into the house of him that sweareth falsely *(and\ or sin)* by my name: and it *(my judgment/ curse/ broken law)*

shall remain in the midst of his house, and shall consume *(destroy)* it with the timber thereof and the stones thereof.

But God chose a better solution for us sinners, which is forgiveness of sin that take away the curse, as follows:

Then the angel that talked with me *(Zechariah)* went forth, and said unto me, Lift up now thine eyes, and see what *is* this that goeth forth.

Zechariah 5:3 through 5:5

These next verses illustrate the portion of an ephah that is the provision(s) being put in place to receive/bear the punishment for the curse (or broken commandments) of God among the nations. This provision from the LORD God shall deliver men from the curse and out of their sin, against Him/His commandments.

Consider Leviticus 5:11; the minimum required, "trespasses in sin", offering which even the poorest sinner could offer during the dispensation of the laws of Moses:

But if he be not able to bring two turtledoves, or two young pigeons, then he that sinned shall bring for his offering the tenth *(10th)* part of an ephah *(or about one tenth bushel)* of fine flour for a sin offering; he shall put no oil upon it, neither shall he put *any* frankincense thereon: for it *is* a sin offering *(or offering for sin)*.

Leviticus 5:11

And I *(Zechariah)* said, What *is* it? And he *(the angel that talked with me)* said, This *is* an ephah *(provision to forgive/atone for sin)* that goeth forth. He said moreover, This *is* their resemblance through all the earth *(or this is what it looks like, and is provided through all the earth?)*.

And, behold, there was lifted up a talent of lead *(representing the weight of the broken Law(s) of God, which is wickedness)*: and this *is* a woman *(not a man, but a woman with her seed)* that sitteth in the midst of the ephah *(provision to forgive sin)*.

And he *(the angel that talked with me)* said, This *(talent of lead) is* wickedness *(or weight of the broken Law(s) of God?)*. And he cast it *(the talent of lead, or weight of the broken Law of God)* into the midst of the ephah *(the minimum provision to forgive sin), the seed of the woman; which seed is Jesus; the grace of God for forgiving sin)*; and he cast the weight of lead upon the mouth *(of the ephah)* thereof *(which silenced the voice of condemnation upon men for the breaking of the Law(s)/ Commandment(s) of God?)*. Recall Romans 8:1, and John 8:11:

Zechariah 5:6 through 5:8

There is therefore now no condemnation to them which are in Christ Jesus, who *(always)* walk not after the flesh, but after the Spirit *(Jesus always walk not after the flesh, but after the Spirit)*.

When Jesus had lifted up himself, and saw none but the woman, he said unto her, Woman, where are those thine accusers? hath no man condemned thee?

She said, No man, Lord. And Jesus said unto her, Neither do I condemn thee: go, and sin no more.

Roman 8:1 and John 8:10 & 8:11

But the commandments of the LORD God shall prevail even among the heathen, according to the provision(s) in Jesus, represented by the ephah; which provision is lifted up between the earth and the heaven in crucifixion, or death!

Then lifted I *(Zechariah)* up mine eyes, and looked, and, behold, there came out two *(2)* women *(Israel and Judah that bear, or birthed Jesus according to the flesh?)*, and the wind *was* in their wings *(the wind representing the Holy Spirit of God)*; for they had wings like the wings of a stork: and they lifted up the ephah *(provision, Jesus, grace of God)* between the earth and the heaven *(in crucifixion!)*.

The permanent place of the provision, or sin bearer of the broken Law(s) of God is established in <u>the rightful</u> place, and even in the wilderness place (Babel/ Babylon/ the world/ Shinar), far above any heathen gods:

Then said I *(Zechariah)* to the angel that talked with me, Whither *(or where)* do these *(two (2) women)* bear the ephah *(provision/ Jesus/ grace of God)*?

And he *(the angel that talked with me)* said unto me, To build it an house in the land of Shinar *(a place above Nebuchadnezzar's false gods. Heretofore, a wilderness and without knowledge of the True God of Creation, but Jesus shall make a place of access to Him/ God; an invite from the LORD God of Creation to the entire world)*: and it *(ephah/ provision/ Jesus/ grace of God)* shall be established, and set there upon her own base *(true principles, foundation, and salvation according to the Gospel). Notice that this verse does not allow us to incorrectly give the seed of man credit; but correctly, the woman's seed for the provision/ ephah/ Jesus/ grace of God to forgive sin: by stating, "and set there upon her own base". This is meaningful because of Genesis 3:14 and 3:15!*

Zechariah 5:9 through 5:11

Reconciliations unto the Atonement

I believe we should be able to get a deeper appreciation for the seriousness the LORD God has for the atonement by the way He dealt with King David's mishandling of it in *2 Samuel Chapter 24 and 1 Chronicles Chapter 21.* Seventy thousand *(70, 000)* men of Israel died as a result of Davis's mishandling!

The Ordinance (law!) that speaks to the reconciliation of humankind unto God through Jesus Christ; for this is introduction to the atonement:

And Aaron shall make an atonement upon the horns of it *(the Altar of Incense?)* once in a year with the blood of the sin offering of atonements:

once in the year shall he make atonement upon it *(the Altar of Incense?)* throughout your generations: it *(the Altar of Incense, and the atonement)* is most holy unto the LORD.

There must also be a "sin offering of atonement" to the LORD when He commands a census be taken of the people! But King David generated lots of trouble for himself and Israel when he commanded a census that was neither sanctioned of God, nor executed properly. Refer to 2Samuel 24:1 and 1Chronicles 21:1.

The reason(s) for King David's census was wrong; and my estimation is that he did it out of pride, and/ or for reason(s) that were not beneficial to all people?

And the LORD spake unto Moses, saying,
Exodus 30:12 describes what David was supposed to do when taking a census:

- When thou takest the sum *(or census)* of the children of Israel after their number, then shall they give every man a ransom *(or sin offering of atonement)* for his soul unto the LORD, when thou numberest *(count)* them *(the children of Israel)*; that there be no plague *(or death)* among them *(the children of Israel)*, when *thou* numberest *(count)* them *(the children of Israel)*.
- This *(ransom)* they shall give, every one that passeth among them that are numbered *(counted)*, half a shekel *(in silver is about 3.61 U.S. dollars today)* after the shekel of the sanctuary *(later the "shekel of the sanctuary" came to be known as the "Temple Tax", which Apostle Peter took from the fish' mouth; Matthew 17:27)*: (a shekel *is* twenty gerahs:) an half shekel *shall be* the offering of *(or given to the Temple for)* the LORD.
- Every one that passeth among them *(the children of Israel)* that are numbered *(counted)*, from twenty years old and above, shall give an offering *(of half a shekel)* unto the LORD *(David also failed to do this. Therefore, the plague upon the people according to the law/ ordinance from Moses, as detailed in Exodus 30:12 above, was one*

of his choices for harsh punishment. And in fact David chose this punishment of the three given, and seventy thousand (70, 000) men died of pestilence; 2Samual 24:15).

The rich shall not give more *(than a half shekel)*, and the poor shall not give less than half a shekel, when *they* give an offering unto the LORD, to make an atonement for your souls. *(All the money/ offering from this were required to be used for the Tabernacle, only! Thus, the whole congregation of the people benefited.)*

And thou shalt take the atonement money of the children of Israel, and shalt appoint it for the service of the tabernacle of the congregation; that it may be a memorial unto the children of Israel before the LORD, to make an atonement for your souls *(mis-handling the census is very, very serious with God because it represents "the reconciliation of God and humankind through Jesus Christ; which is the atonement").*

Exodus 30:10 through 30:16

The Abomination of Desolation

Without doubt most of us can see how Cain's mishandling of the sacrifice *(atonement)* by his offering in **Genesis 4:3 through 4:8** were offensive to the LORD God.

But, how many people do you suppose that lived from the time of Moses unto the Lord Jesus Christ really understood the seriousness of the offense to God for King David's mishandling of the atonement? Or even the more serious offense of what Antiochus IV Epiphanies so hatefully did when he sacrificed a pig on the Altar in Jerusalem, as detailed in **Daniel 11:21 through 11:35?** And secular history also recorded it *(the abomination)*!

And even for us today; do we really understand the seriousness of the offense to God for rejecting Jesus *(not just the figures of Him in the Old Testament, but the actual atonement: Jesus and Him crucified on the cross!)*? Even so, some will still ask the question, "how is rejecting Jesus deserving of hell?" But then another question arises: "where else would

God put those that rejected/ don't want any part with Him"? This is His Universe, but your decisions say you want nothing to do with Him and His preeminence! *He has set the table for a feast, invited everyone; but many have rejected it!* Folks this is rebellion against <u>The Creator</u>, and I am persuaded there comes a time when ignorance is no longer an excuse, and the question becomes "why don't you understand? You seem to have sufficient curiosity for investigating things that concern you"! **This concerns you!**

But just like, and in the same way as Satan and those with him rebelled against the Creator in the ancient past, and continues to rebel, the human race has done the very same things!

If Satan, the devil, can be God as was boasted in *Ezekiel Chapter 28*, why does he not create his own universe, or creation? Why does he contend/ resist God for control of this one? Have you ever thought about that?

And so, what about you too; do your ways declare you do not want anything to do with God, the Creator?

But concerning David, let us not forget to mention though, how much his heart convicted him when the prophet Gad explained the seriousness of the situation due to his *(David's)* actions in *2Samuel Chapter 24 and 1Chronicles Chapter 21*! It would be good for us too, if we gained such revelation(s) of needed deliverance!

And there remains another "abomination of desolation" in prophecy yet to be fulfilled. The Prophet Daniel spoke of this other abomination also, in Daniel 12:11:

> Dan 12:11 And from the time *that* the daily *sacrifice* shall be taken away, and the abomination that maketh desolate set up, *there shall be* a thousand two hundred and ninety *(1290)* days.

Dan 12:12 Blessed *is* he that waiteth, and cometh to the thousand three hundred and five and thirty *(1335)* days *(or 45 days after the 1290 is completed!)*.

Dan 12:13 But go thou thy way *(Daniel)* till the end *be*: for thou shalt rest, and stand in thy lot at the end of the days *(or end time)*.

Jesus spoke of this very same prophecy, when He talked about the man of sin during end times tribulations in Matthew 24:15 and Mark 13:14.

Mat 24:15 When ye therefore shall see the abomination of desolation, spoken of by Daniel the prophet, stand in the holy place, (whoso readeth, let him understand:)

Mar 13:14 But when ye shall see the abomination of desolation, spoken of by Daniel the prophet, standing where it ought not, (let him that readeth understand,) then let them that be in Judaea flee to the mountains:

Now, using your Judeo – Christian Bible read those verses leading up to, and the subsequent verses of Matthew 24:15, and Mark 13:14. Also, read Chapter 14 of Zechariah to get a full picture, in prophecy, of what these references say shall happen at that time. But if your situation is that you have no personal Judeo – Christian Bible, those scripture texts have been provided, with our comments, after this next paragraph!

The man of sin, as referred to by scripture, shall take up position in the holy place, claiming to be God; therefore claiming to be the atonement, and the author of the atonement: Thus, he is an abomination (i.e., a creature claiming himself his own creator; but it is God that has created him), and his claim is desolate (impossible to ever have been accomplished then, or at any other time)!

I am not sure if anyone can begin to understand the offense to the True God of Creation, the abomination of desolation this man of sin shall manifest!

===========================

Matthew 24 Verses 1 through 44 (Prophesies Given By the Lord Jesus Christ)

Jerusalem Shall Be Destroyed By the Romans

Luke 19:37 through 19:44 says Judah of Israel did not recognize the time of their "visitation"!

I am persuaded this is the time God wanted to restore Israel such that the past 1987 years (2017 A.D. – 30 A.D.) would have been their evangelizing of Gentiles, rather than the object of so much ridicule and destruction from the Gentiles:

And when he *(Jesus)* was come nigh, even now at the descent of the mount of Olives, the whole multitude of the disciples began to rejoice and praise God with a loud voice for all the mighty works that they had seen **(which Jesus performed, and Moses pointed to as signs of Messiah in Deuteronomy 18:15 through 18:22)**;

Saying, Blessed *be* the King **(Jesus is the King)** that cometh in the name of the Lord: peace in heaven, and glory in the highest **(This is also that prophecy of Deuteronomy 18:15 through 18:22 being fulfilled, just as God promised by Moses!)**.

And some of the Pharisees **(in disagreement)** from among the multitude said unto him **(Jesus)**, Master, rebuke thy disciples **(for saying "Blessed be the King that cometh in the name of the Lord: peace in heaven, and glory in the highest")**.

And he **(Jesus)** answered and said unto them **(the disagreeable Pharisees)**, I tell you that, if these **(the disciples that praised him (Jesus as King) along side of heaven)** should hold their peace, the stones would immediately cry out **(and say the truth, if the disciple had refuse to say what they knew to be true)**.

And when he *(Jesus)* was come near, he beheld the city, and wept over it,

Saying, If thou **(Judah of Israel)** hadst known, even thou, at least in this thy day, the things *which belong* unto thy peace! but now they are hid from thine eyes **(because you have rejected me; your salvation!)**.

(The prophecy of these next two verses took on a new seriousness when Rome destroyed the City and Temple at Jerusalem in 70 A.D. Since then the Jews have been scattered throughout the nations; singled out and killed for centuries. But in 1948 A.D. the LORD God began collecting them (His remnant of Israel) into a nation again as declared according to Bible Prophecy).

For the days shall come upon thee, that thine enemies shall cast a trench about thee, and compass thee round, and keep thee in on every side,
And shall lay thee even with the ground, and thy children within thee; and they shall not leave in thee one stone upon another; because thou knewest not the time of thy visitation *(the coming, presence, and fulfilling of Messiah, Jesus; the LORD among them)*.
Luke 19:37 through 19:44

Jesus prophesies of the, "70 A.D. destruction" of the Temple, and Jerusalem, and ensuing wars against Israel unto the time of his 2nd coming:

And Jesus went out, and departed from the temple: and his disciples came to *him* for to shew him the buildings of the temple.
And Jesus said unto them, See ye not all these things? Verily I say unto you, There shall not be left here one stone upon another, that shall not be thrown down.
And as he sat upon the mount of Olives, the disciples came unto him privately, saying, Tell us, when shall these things be? And what *shall be* the sign of thy *(next, or 2nd)* coming, and of the end of the world?
And Jesus answered and said unto them, Take heed that no man deceive you.
For many shall come in my name, saying, I am Christ; and shall deceive many.
And ye shall hear of wars and rumours of wars: see that ye be not troubled: for all *these things* must come to pass, but the end is not yet.
For nation shall rise against nation *(civil wars)*, and kingdom against kingdom *(wars of kingdom against another kingdom)*: and there shall be famines, and pestilences, and earthquakes, in divers places.
All these *are* the beginning of sorrows.

Then shall they deliver you *(the people of God)* up to be afflicted, and shall kill you: and ye shall be hated of all nations for my name's sake.
And then shall many be offended, and shall betray one another, and shall hate one another.
And many false prophets shall rise, and shall deceive many.
And because iniquity shall abound, the love of many shall wax cold.
But he that shall endure unto the end *(or until my 2nd coming)*, the same shall be saved.
And this gospel of the kingdom shall be preached in all the world for a witness unto all nations; and then shall the end come.

Matthew 24:1 through 24:14

Jesus Prophesy of His Second Coming

When ye *(National Israel)* therefore shall see the abomination of desolation, spoken of by Daniel the prophet, stand in the holy place, (whoso readeth, let him understand,) ... then let them which be in Judea flee into the mountains. *(In other words; when Judah, the National remnant of Israel, eventually "recognizes the abomination of desolation" standing on the Temple Mount in Jerusalem as "abomination of desolation" ... then the time clock of Daniel's 70-weeks shall resume!*
Question: Has part of the abomination of desolation been standing in the holy place (Jerusalem Temple Mount) since the Muslim temple was built there about 600 A.D.; and the other part is that of 2 Thessalonians 2:5 through 2:12?)

Matthew 24:15

The context of this prophecy must be considered on the time line of Daniels 70 weeks alone, which does not include, or the Church age is not part. Refer to, "The Prophecy of Daniel Chapter 9".

And from the time *that* the daily *sacrifice* shall be taken away *(the event of the sacrifice of Jesus, or the 69 ½ week of Daniels 70 weeks)*, and the abomination that maketh desolate set up *(man of sin declare himself God?)*, *there shall be* a thousand two hundred and ninety *(1290)* days *(or then this shall begins the final ½ week of Daniel's 70th week, after the Church's rapture?).*

Blessed *is* he *(Jesus, Messiah, Atoning Sacrifice, and King)* that waiteth, and cometh *(2nd coming)* to the thousand three hundred and five and thirty *(1335)* days *(which is 45 days later than 1290 days).*
Daniel 12:11 through 12:12

This next series of scriptures (Matthew 24:16 through 24:31) is considered to be the time of the Battle of Armageddon? Also see Ezekiel Chapters 38 and 39, Zechariah Chapter 14, Revelation 11:15 through 11:19, Revelation 16:16, Revelation 19:11 through 19:21. These are all the same approximate time frame, or "season"!

Then let them which be in Judaea flee into the mountains:
Let him which is on the housetop not come down to take any thing out of his house:
Neither let him which is in the field return back to take his clothes.
And woe unto them that are with child, and to them that give suck in those days *(perhaps, since any travel shall be so difficult because of the times; the distance, being filled with obstacles/checkpoints, shall be many days and hours?)*!
But pray ye that your flight be not in the winter, neither on the Sabbath day:
For then shall be great tribulation, such as was not since the beginning of the world to this time, no, nor ever shall be.
And except those days should be shortened, there should no flesh be saved: but for the elect's sake those days shall be shortened *(The elect is thought to be the remnant of Judah that Jesus returned this 2nd time to save, and any Gentile converts gained to the kingdom of God since the rapture!).*
Then if any man shall say unto you, Lo, here *is* Christ, or there; believe *it* not.
For there shall arise false Christs, and false prophets, and shall shew great signs and wonders; insomuch that, if *it were* possible, they

shall deceive the very elect *(only if it be possible to deceive the elect! Perhaps the LORD shall not allow it to be possible?)*.

Behold, I have told you before *(during other conversations)*.

Wherefore if they shall say unto you, Behold, he is in the desert; go not forth: behold, *he is* in the secret chambers; believe *it* not.

For as the lightning cometh out of the east, and shineth even unto the west; so shall also the coming of the Son of man be *(He shall come out of the direction of the rising sun, and He shall catch, or snatch His people to Him!)*.

For wheresoever the carcase is, there will the eagles *(fleshing eating birds, and buzzards)* be gathered together.

Immediately after the tribulation of those days shall the sun be darkened, and the moon shall not give her light, and the stars shall fall from heaven, and the powers of the heavens *(spiritual authorities; speaks of anti-Christ(s), fallen angels, demons, and/ or Satan?)* shall be shaken:

And then shall appear the sign of the Son of man in heaven: and then shall all the tribes *(nations)* of the earth mourn, and they shall see the Son of man coming in the clouds of heaven with power and great glory.

And he shall send his angels with a great sound of a trumpet, and they shall gather together his elect from the four winds, from one end of heaven to the other *(this seems to be different than the rapture, which shall be like as a thief in the night. A great sound of a trumpet marks this event, here!)*.

Matthew 24:16 through 24:31

Signs of the Time of the Return of Christ Jesus

Now learn a parable of the fig tree *(the fig tree, Israel was established again after WWII in 1948 A.D.)*; When his branch *(the fig tree\ Judah of Israel)* is yet tender, and putteth forth leaves, ye know that summer *is* nigh *(or what condition(s) is nigh\ about to occur? The 100 year mark of the fig tree (Israel) is 2048 A.D.)*:

So likewise ye, when ye shall see all these things, know that it *(the tribulation and 2nd coming of Jesus)* is near, *even* at the doors.

Verily I say unto you, This generation *(the generation that witnesses the beginning signs of the time of the fig tree and return of Jesus?)* shall not pass, till all these things be fulfilled.

Heaven and earth shall pass away, but my words shall not pass away.

But of that *(exact?)* day and hour knoweth no *man,* no, not the angels of heaven, but my Father only *(but we are encouraged to discern the season(s) of the times, and be ready).*

But as the days of Noe *(Noah) were,* so shall also the coming of the Son of man be.

For as in the days that were before the flood they were eating and drinking, marrying and giving in marriage *(or their daily living same as any other day),* until the day that Noe *(Noah)* entered into the ark *(or, the Church rapture; which entering the ark that saved Noah and his family, is the type, Don't You See?),*

And knew not until the flood *(2nd return of Jesus; marked first, or signaled by the great earthquake of Revelation 6:12; rather than a flood in the case of Noah?)* came, and took them all away; so shall also the coming of the Son of man be.

Mat 24:40 Then shall two *(men?)* be in the field; the one shall be taken *(perish in the earthquake, or taken to safety in the rapture?),* and the other left *(to go through the tribulation?).*

Mat 24:41 Two *women shall be* grinding at the mill; the one shall be taken *(perish in the earthquake, or taken to safety in the rapture?),* and the other left *(to go through the tribulation?)*

(Question 1: Are these two verses of Matthew 24:40 and 24:41 telling us that where as all the souls of Noah's day were lost except for eight (8) people (Noah and his family); the souls that shall be lost (or not entered into safety of the rapture\ Ark) at the beginning of the tribulation (Revelation 6:12) to be followed by the 2nd return of Jesus as described in (Revelation 11:15 through 11:19, Revelation 16:16, Revelation 19:11 through 19:21, Ezekiel Chapters 38 and 39, Zechariah Chapter 14) shall be greater than fifty percent (50%: One taken, the other left)? Thus, the fate of the one taken shall be "safety

in the rapture", or "death by earthquake"! The estimate of people on earth in 2015 A.D. was about seven billion three hundred million (7.3 billion)! If Matthew 24:40 and 24:41 had occurred in 2015 A.D., then 3.65 billion people would have remained on earth to experience the tribulation!

Question 2: So, how many of the remaining folks (50%), on earth, of that day (after Revelation 6:12) would you suppose shall be concerned whether the rapture had taken place: Or Not?

Question 3: Shall we dare imagine that modern conveniences would return to pre-horse and buggy days, because of such great devastation(s) upon infrastructure, brought on by the Revelation 6:12 earthquake?

This earthquake (not the climate!) shall be "just the beginning of the tribulation"! However, the climate shall indeed be impacted.).

Watch therefore: for ye know not what hour your Lord doth come.

But know this, that if the goodman of the house had known in what watch the thief would come, he would have watched, and would not have suffered his house to be broken up.

Therefore be ye also ready *(because you now know the season began at the re-establishing of National Israel; Judah, the remnant people of God?)*: for in such an hour as ye think not the Son of man cometh.

Matthew 24:32 through 24:44

===========================

Zechariah Chapter 14

The Day of the LORD Jesus, and the Time of His Second (2nd) Coming

Behold, the day of the LORD cometh, and thy *(Judah of Israel's)* spoil *(remaining possession/ habitation?)* shall be divided in the midst of thee.

This prophecy, I believe, includes the time of the Battle of Armageddon, because the LORD says in Zechariah 14:2, He "will gather all nations against Jerusalem". Therefore this prophecy, do not seem to be about the destruction of Jerusalem by the Roman Empire in 70 A.D.!

Also, the day of the LORD shall be the time, "his feet shall stand in that day upon the mount of Olives", as described in Zechariah 14:4 and 14:5.

For I will gather all nations against Jerusalem to battle; and the city shall be taken, and the houses rifled, and the women ravished; and half of the city *(as described in 14:1 above?)* shall go forth into captivity, and the residue of the people shall not be cut off from the city. Then shall the LORD *(Jesus)* go forth, and fight against those nations, as when he fought in the day of battle *(in my mind this raises the question as to whether this is referring to the Book of Joshua, verses 5:13 through 5:15, as listed below?).*
Zechariah 14:1 through 14:3

At first glance these verses of Joshua 5:13 through 5:15 would seem to be about Michael; the LORD'S Chief Angel of War that appears to Joshua before his greatest battles? But the man said to Joshua the same words that were said to Moses on Mount Sinai out of the burning bush! Therefore, I am persuaded this is not Michael; but, is this the LORD Jesus incarnate? Also, would Michael, being and angel, receive worship?

And it came to pass, when Joshua was by Jericho, that he lifted up his eyes and looked, and, behold, there stood a man over against him with his sword drawn in his hand: and Joshua went unto him, and said unto him, *Art* thou for us, or for our adversaries?

And he *(the man with the sword)* said, Nay; but *as* captain of the host of the LORD am I now come. And Joshua fell on his face to the earth, and did worship, and said unto him, What saith my lord unto his servant?

And the captain of the LORD'S host said unto Joshua, Loose thy shoe from off thy foot; for the place whereon thou standest *is* holy. And Joshua did so.

Here is another thought about this subject, which we should consider:

There exists the notion that Joshua is a type and figure of the Lord Jesus Christ, when He fight for Israel at his "second coming", that they (Israel) be not destroyed at the Battle of Armageddon (Revelation 16:16).

The type and figure also, is that the Lord Jesus shall defend Israel in the very "Land of Promise" Joshua fights for in the Book of Joshua! But the corpses and carnage resulting from Jesus defending Israel shall be worse than anything before, and ever shall be again! Also see Ezekiel Chapters 38 and 39, Zechariah 14:1 through 14:3, Revelation 11:15 through 11:19, Revelation 19:11 through 19:21. I am persuaded all of these scripture references are pointing to related, and perhaps, the very same event(s) of end times!

Joshua 5:13 through 5:15

The very specific point in time of the second coming of the Lord Jesus Christ is described in this next verse of Zechariah 14:4?

And his feet shall stand in that day upon the mount of Olives, which *is* before Jerusalem on the east, and the mount of Olives shall cleave *(split)* in the midst thereof toward the east and toward the west, *and there shall be* a very great valley; and half of the mountain *(Mount of Olives)* shall remove toward the north, and half of it toward the south *(in other words the LORD Jesus shall cause a rift/ valley from* east to west upon the Mount of Olives when He set foot there upon His return. Also a mountain on the north side and south side of the valley shall be formed as a result!).*

And ye *(Judah of Israel)* shall flee *to* the valley of the mountains *(Jesus created by the splitting of the Mount of Olives)*; for the valley *(splitting of the Mount of Olives)* of the mountains shall reach unto Azal *(Wadi Yasul, or Nahal Azal?)*: yea, ye *(Judah of Israel)* shall flee, like as ye fled from before the earthquake in the days of Uzziah king of Judah: and the LORD my God shall come, *and* all the saints with thee *(thus, rapture(s) of some fashion must have taken place before this incident, because all the saints are with him at the time of this event of Zechariah 14:5?).*

Only the LORD knows when this day shall occur:

This shall also be the time that, the reign/ rule of kingdoms by men on earth are fully removed/ rescinded/ taken away/ discontinued, since the time of Genesis 1:26!

And it shall come to pass in that day, *that* the light *(sun and moon?)* shall not be clear, *nor* dark:

But it shall be one day which shall be known *(when, only)* to the LORD, not day, nor night: but it shall come to pass, *that* at evening time it shall be light *(Shall this day of, "not day, nor night" be so, because of the presence of the LORD, or a change of earth's axis resulting from Zechariah 14:4 and 14:5, or both?).*

And it shall be in that day, *that* living waters *(from the LORD?)* shall go out from Jerusalem; half of them *(living waters?)* toward the former *(or dead?)* sea, and half of them toward the hinder *(or Mediterranean?)* sea: in summer and in winter *(or year round)* shall it be *(also refer to Ezekiel 47:1 through 47:12).*

And the LORD shall be king over all the earth: in that day shall there be one LORD, and his name one *(the great, "I AM"?).*

All the land shall be turned as a plain *(or made flat?)* from Geba to Rimmon south of Jerusalem: and it shall be lifted up *(raised in sea level?)*, and inhabited in her place, from Benjamin's gate unto the place of the first gate, unto the corner gate, and *from* the tower of Hananeel unto the king's winepresses.

And *men* shall dwell in it, and there shall be no more utter destruction; but Jerusalem shall be safely inhabited.

Zechariah 14:4 through 14:11

The prophecy of more events in the day of the LORD:

And this shall be the plague wherewith the LORD will smite all the people that have fought against Jerusalem; Their flesh shall consume away while they stand upon their feet, and their eyes shall consume away in their holes *(or sockets)*, and their tongue shall consume away in their mouth.

And it shall come to pass in that day, *that* a great tumult *(noisome commotion?)* from the LORD shall be among them; and they shall lay hold every one on the hand of his neighbour, and his hand shall rise up against the hand of his neighbour.

And Judah also shall fight at Jerusalem; and the wealth of all the heathen round about shall be gathered together, gold, and silver, and apparel, in great abundance.

And so shall be the plague of the horse, of the mule, of the camel, and of the ass, and of all the beasts that shall be in these tents, as this plague *(even the animals owned of the enemies of the people of God shall have the same fate as their masters!)*.

Zechariah 14:16

And it shall come to pass, *that* every one that is left of all the nations which came against Jerusalem shall even go up from year to year to worship the King, the LORD of hosts, and to keep the feast of tabernacles *(booths/ sukkot/ ingathering)*.

It is important we know that a Jewish Temple must be in place at Jerusalem in order to "correctly" celebrate the feast of tabernacles.

The LORD God has permitted no Jewish temple building at Jerusalem since the Roman destruction in 70 A.D. Thus, the question arises: how can celebration of this feast be rightly accomplished today, during the Church

age, since animal sacrifices "seemingly" must be part of the celebration? I say this because some Christian (and none Christian!) Organizations apparently believe we are in error, not to conduct this celebration.

Then, another question arises, whether this verse of Zechariah's prophecy is, at all, to the Church?

If we study Zechariah 14:5 closely, it seems the time of the events of this verse (Zechariah 14:16) is post Church Age, or post rapture? But, of course, there are also those who say there shall not occur, such an event as, "the rapture"? I would recommend to anyone that is really concerned: "diligently study for yourself, and ask the Holy Spirit for guidance on this subject" before deciding.

In addition, consider this: Jesus shall reign from Jerusalem in the post Church age and beyond, and He is both living sacrifice and living temple: He is the atonement!

Because of this prophecy of Zechariah 14:16 some conclude (I think incorrectly) that the LORD God shall command animal sacrificial ordinances of Moses to be resumed in Jerusalem at some point in time and continued during the millennial reign? My response to this notion is a resounding, "Not so fast my brother(s) and sister(s)"! The explanation for this is as follows:

The requirement(s) Moses and those after him were to make animal sacrifices by way of the tabernacle/ temple; atoning for sin(s) of the people unto reconciling with God. Jesus fulfilled this for all times by His sacrificial death on the cross and He subsequently arose from the dead. He is now the "living" Tabernacle, Temple, and the living Sacrifice! Therefore, when Jesus is in Jerusalem, or anywhere else for that matter, "He is the Tabernacle, Temple, and the Sacrifice" for every purpose God intended! So then, who else, or what else "greater" would one suppose God requires for man's reconciliation, anywhere, anytime?

Folks, for us today the eternal reconciliation is accomplished (made, done, completed, finished, nothing else to be done). All we need do is thank and praise God for it, believe it, receive it, and take part in it (or take part of it), Forever! No new sacrificial tabernacles, temples, or sacrifices are required (Don't You See)!

I am persuaded if such a thing is attempted it will not be because the LORD God commissioned, or said to do it; Amen!

But now of course, men have always done things God has not said they should do, and things He has said to do, they (we) often leave undone; even the children of Israel, "instructed of Moses" in the wilderness encountered this problem of disobedience, time after time, after time. And in Old and New Testament Scripture we see there comes a time when the LORD God allows us to have just what we so tirelessly insist upon having; whether good, or bad! John 3:16 is the simplest illustration of this; would you not agree?

Zechariah 14:12 through 14:16

This shall also be the time of the sheep and goat nations as prophesied in Matthew 25:31 through 25:46!

> And it shall be, *that* whoso will not come up of *all* the families of the earth unto Jerusalem to worship the King, the LORD of hosts, even upon them shall be no rain *(as in water!)*.
> And if the family of Egypt *(or the world)* go not up, and come not, that *have* no *rain;* there shall be the plague, wherewith the LORD will smite the heathen that come not up to keep the feast of tabernacles.
> This shall be the punishment of Egypt *(and, or the world?)*, and the punishment of all nations that come not up to keep the feast of tabernacles.
> In that day shall there be upon the bells of the horses, HOLINESS UNTO THE LORD; and the pots *(cooking utensils?)* in the LORD'S house shall be like *(or have the same purpose as?)* the

bowls *(drink offering utensils?)* before the altar *(because Jesus will have fulfilled all these things!)*.

Yea, every pot in Jerusalem and in Judah shall be holiness unto the LORD of hosts: and all they that sacrifice shall come and take of them, and seethe therein: and in that day there shall be no more the Canaanite *(false god/idol worshiper)* in the house of the LORD of hosts.

Zechariah 14:17 through 14:21

DEFINITIONS & FIGURES

Agape Love – First *(1ˢᵗ)* Corinthians Chapter 13:

This Chapter 13 of 1 Corinthians is often referred to as Paul's Chapter on charity, or love. Love that pleases God fulfills the law unto justification (Romans 13:8 through 13:10).

Though I speak with the tongues of men and of *(or about)* angels, and have not charity *(or love)*, I am become *as* sounding brass, or a tinkling cymbal *(in other words it is like talking to hear yourself talk, and there is nothing of your real intent and concern in it)*.

And though I have *the gift of* prophecy, and understand all mysteries, and all knowledge; and though I have all faith, so that I could remove mountains, and have not charity, I am nothing.

And though I bestow all my goods to feed *the poor,* and though I give my body to be burned, and have not charity, it profiteth me nothing *(notice Paul does not say doing all these things profits no one else nothing; but it profit me nothing if I am doing these things without being motivated of love)*.

Charity suffereth long *(or put up with stuff that opposes it), and* is kind; charity envieth not *(or is not resentful)*; charity vaunteth *(boast)* not itself, is not puffed up *(not full of self pride)*,

Doth not behave itself unseemly *(not inappropriately, but according to decency of respect unto God?)*, seeketh not her own *(do not defend itself at the expense of another, nor the defenseless)*, is not easily provoked *(angered)*, thinketh no evil *(allow one that is accused, forgiveness, and seek not revenge)*;

Rejoiceth not in iniquity *(immorality)*, but rejoiceth in the truth *(and that which is right)*;

(Charity, or love) Beareth all things, believeth all things, hopeth all things, endureth all things.

Charity never faileth *(or withdraw from its own attribute of, "charity"?)*: but whether *there be* prophecies, they shall fail; whether *there be* tongues, they shall cease; whether *there be* knowledge, it shall vanish away.

For we know in part, and we prophesy in part *(because we are not yet mature)*.

But when that which is perfect *(fully mature)* is come, then that which is in part *(lack maturity)* shall be done away.

When I was a child, I spake as a child *(or in part)*, I understood as a child *(or in part)*, I thought as a child *(or in part)*: but when I became a man *(mature in Jesus Christ)*, I put away childish things *(or knowing in part)*.

For now *(in this time of childhood)* we see *(as)* through a glass, darkly; but then *(when perfect, or maturity is come)* face to face: now I know in part *(or as a child)*; but then *(when perfect, or maturity is come)* shall I know *(God?)* even as also I am known *(of God?)*.

And *(for)* now *(as I am yet a child)* abideth faith, hope, charity, these three; but the greatest of these *is* charity *(or love)*.

1 Corinthians 13:1 through 13:13

Apocrypha Books – Perhaps the argument can be made that the commandment from Moses, in the ***Book of Deuteronomy, Verses 17:14 through 17:20*** might be a contributing factor to the productions of so many "stand alone" Judeo – Christian works that were not included with the official, "Canon of Scripture"! Such writings have been assigned the category of, *"Apocrypha Books"*.

Even though the commandment is specifically for the king of Israel, Moses does not exclude any other persons *(whether just curious, dedicated, or otherwise)* about God; from attempting the very same task of copying scripture texts! For example, there are a few Psalms not written by the king!

But the Holy Spirit superintended, and had final say of the writings that constitute the Canon of Scripture available for us today, which consist of the Old and New Testaments *(described primarily by the King James, and documentations used to develop the King James (i.e., the King James seems to be the most widely used). Zechariah 4:6 is one of our many witnesses in scripture that God bring to past what He does by His Spirit; the Holy Spirit)*!

When the people of Israel decided they wanted a king in Israel, rather than the LORD God in single authority over them:

When thou art come unto the land which the LORD thy God giveth thee, and shalt possess it, and shalt dwell therein, and shalt say, I will set a king over me, like as all the nations that *are* about me *(by the way the nations round about them were false god and idol worshipers; or heathens!)*;

Thou shalt in any wise set *him* king over thee, whom the LORD thy God shall choose: *one* from among thy brethren shalt thou set king over thee: thou mayest not set a stranger over thee, which *is* not thy brother *(or not from the line of Jacob)*.

But he shall not multiply horses to himself, nor cause the people to return to Egypt, to the end that he should multiply horses: forasmuch as the LORD hath said unto you, Ye shall henceforth return no more that way *(to Egypt, which are worshippers of many false gods and idols)*.

Neither shall he multiply wives to himself, that his heart turn not away *(from the LORD God of his fathers; Abraham, Isaac, and Jacob)*: neither shall he greatly multiply to himself silver and gold *(that he turns away from trusting the LORD God)*.

And it shall be, when he sitteth upon the throne of his kingdom, that he shall write him a copy of this law in a book out of *that which is* before the priests the Levites *(in other words the King in Israel shall write his own copy of the Bible, <u>based upon</u>, or using the existing books that is with the priesthood)*:

And it *(the copy of his (the Kings) Bible that he writes)* shall be with him, and he shall read therein all the days of his life: that he may learn to fear the LORD his God, to keep all the words of this law and these statutes, to do them:

That his heart be not lifted up above his brethren *(or those he is king over)*, and that he turn not aside from the commandment, *to* the right hand, or *to* the left: to the end that he may prolong *his* days in his kingdom, he, and his children, in the midst of Israel.

Deuteronomy 17:14 through 17:20

Area of King Saul's Territory – The solid **boundary** line inside the map figure provides approximate area of Israel at the death of King Saul. But this is smaller than the greater borders the LORD God promised Abraham in Genesis 15:17 through 15:21. The rule of Saul began about *1104 B.C.* He reigned about forty years *(40)* until about *1064 B.C. (Acts 13:21).*

Behemoth – Obviously, no living animal fitting the description provided in *Job 40:15* inhabits the earth today! The best secular estimation(s) of "why not" has been, "the changing climate conditions" Thus, the climate has always changed; and therefore, these size animals could no longer be supported by the changing ecosystem!

In my opinion, no natural human element(s) contributed to the "Behemoth's" extinction! It seems the LORD God made the Behemoth, which *Job 40:15 through 40:24* describes, for a specific period in time. Its description does seem to fit that of many species of dinosaur we are taught about today, according to fossil record. But in no way does the description resemble that of an elephant; the largest living land animal we know exists in our time! Also refer to our statement about "Leviathan", which *Job 41:1 through 41:34* describes.

Leviathan – We can say similar things about this sea creature as we did about the "Behemoth land creature" of *Job 40:15 through 40:24*! This creature too, "the Leviathan" is obviously extinct: That is, climate conditions became more and more unfavorable for supporting its diet, and required habitat. Human influence *(i.e., carbon foot print)* upon the climate of that time would have been negligible, since there was no combustible machinery, or industrial manufacturing, etc.! And so we surmise; the climate has always been in a state of "change"; without human intervention.

But there seems to be many people among the citizenry today that believe technology will eventually make the climate behave according to their prescribed and desired pattern(s)! I am of the mind that technology can have a local climate impact, but making the climate behave as one will for the long term, shall not happen any time soon, since the Sun, other Solar System bodies, and volcanic activity on the planet are known to be major contributors to the climate!

The LORD God made the leviathan, which *Job 41:1 through 41:34* described to be a dragon, as I see it; and thought to be an "ancient myth" by most folks today. The fact that it is a sea dwelling creature may explain why no fossil record has ever been uncovered, or seen of it during this modern age! *Job 41:9* seems to imply that this creature was already becoming extinct according to the time, and context God described, and as the Book of Job portrayed.

The description of this ancient animal is not that of a smooth skinned whale; the largest living sea dweller we know exists, solely in the sea today!

Borders of Israel When Joshua Died – This map provides approximate boundaries, and locations of Israel's inheritance according to the Book of Numbers Chapter 34, and Deuteronomy Chapter 34:1 through 34:4. But this is smaller than the greater borders the LORD God promised Abraham in Genesis 15:17 through 15:21 *(an approximate estimate of Joshua's death would be 1445 to 1450 B.C.)*.

Borders of David's Kingdom – The shaded area adjacent to the Mediterranean Sea indicate the borders established of David, as the LORD God made him victorious over all his enemies. These borders are more in line with the promise God gave Abraham in Genesis 15:17 through 15:21, than any other borders declared to be controlled by the children of Israel before David *(his reign was about 1064 to 1024 B.C.)*.

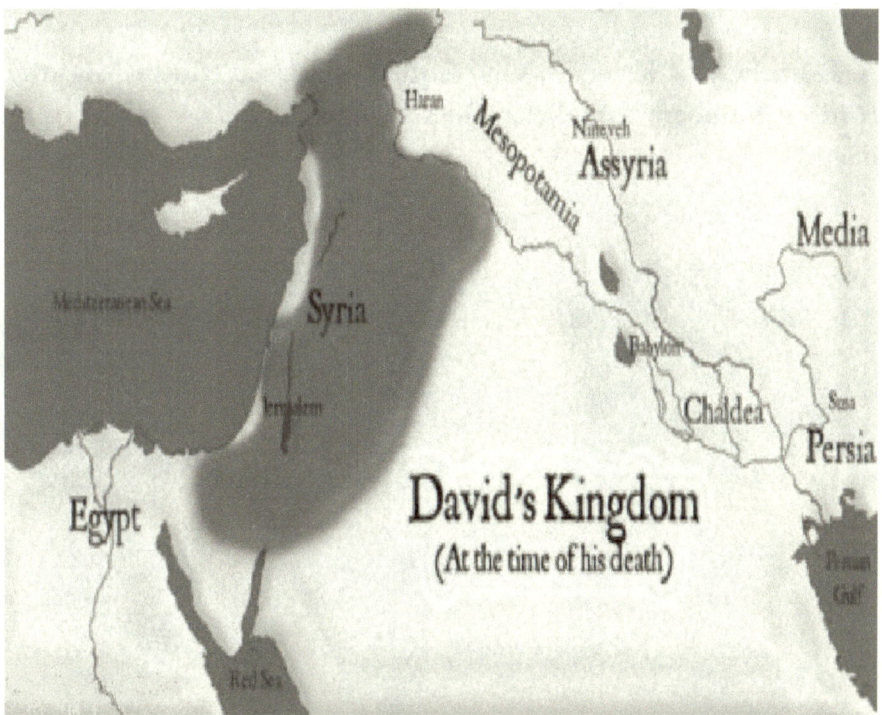

Border of Inheritance – The **boundary** line along the Mediterranean Sea, and extending in land to include the areas of Canaanites, Kenites, Jebusites, Ammonites, and Kadonites provides approximate boundaries of Israel's inheritance according to Numbers Chapter 34. But even this is smaller than the greater borders the LORD God promised Abraham in Genesis 15:17 through 15:21. The cover of our Book on Numbers with the title & subtitle:

A Testimony of Jesus 13: God Called and Used Moses Mightily (Moses Numbers' Israel), provides an expanded view of this map image.

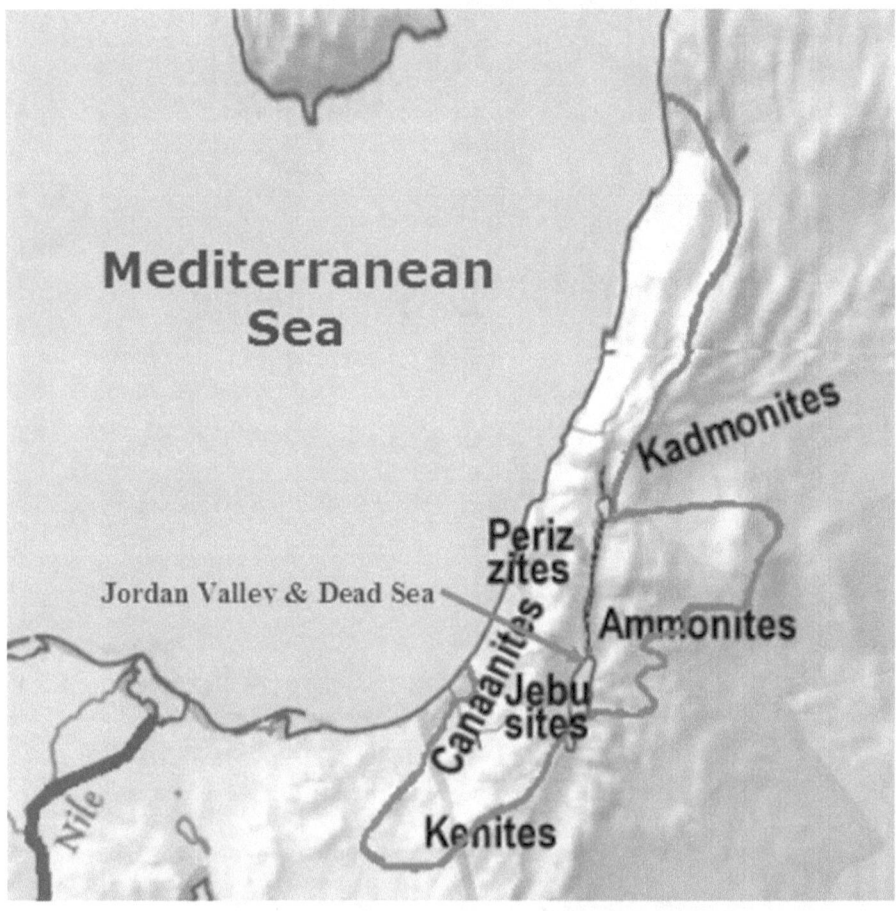

Born Again, and Redeemed - *Why do you think your ways are beyond or better than those of the LORD God of Creation?*

Isa 40:27 Why sayest thou, O Jacob *(or sons of Jacob)*, and speakest, O Israel, *(that)* My way is hid from *(or is unknown to)* the LORD *(God)*, and my judgment is passed over from *(or above that of)* my God? *(Why do you say this is the twenty first (21ˢᵗ) century; God is out dated, or God needs help with His program, let us show Him how things ought to be and really are!?*

Did you know there is no malice on the part of the mad dog's behavior? No consideration for what is right, or wrong; no love; not even hate! He's just being what he is, A MAD DOG! And in order to determine what makes it "a mad dog" one must look further, because it was not born "a mad dog".

But although redeemable, since God *(in the beginning)* created human kind akin to Himself; the *(human being in the eyes of God)* is born that way of *(sin resulting in a death sentence)*, and must be "born again"; else the LORD God of Creation has no <u>USEFUL</u>, <u>LASTING</u> purpose to assign *(the unredeemed individual)* in His Universe!

However, the dog never ever can be redeemed *(whether mad or sane)*; not ever having been akin to God *(for God is Spirit and eternal)*. In other words the appearing of a specific dog on the stage of creation is a one time deal; there can be another one like it, but not that one!

And so, the human individual if not having been "born again"; has the same status as the dog before the eyes of the *perfect LORD and God of Creation.*

Only a few with Noah, and the children of Israel were given redeemable assurance before the appearing of Jesus, and His sacrificial crucifixion; which was necessary, saves us and them of old, according to faith and promise! *(Refer to Matthew 15:21 through 15:28; John 3:1 through 3:12; 1Peter 1:17 through 1:25) as follows:*

Matthew 15 – The dog in the eyes of the LORD God:

Mat 15:21 Then Jesus went thence, and departed into the coasts of Tyre and Sidon.

Mat 15:22 And, behold, a woman of Canaan came out of the same coasts, and cried unto him, saying, Have mercy on me, O Lord, *thou* Son of David; my daughter is grievously vexed with a devil.

Mat 15:23 But he *(Jesus)* answered her not a word. And his disciples came and besought him *(Jesus)*, saying, Send her *(the Gentile woman of Canaan)* away; for she crieth *(or bother)* after us.

Mat 15:24 But he *(Jesus)* answered and said, I am not sent but unto the lost sheep of the house of Israel.

Mat 15:25 Then came she *(the Gentile woman of Canaan)* and worshipped him *(Jesus)*, saying, Lord, help me.

Mat 15:26 But he *(Jesus)* answered and said, It is not meet *(or the right thing to do)* to take the children's bread, and to cast *it* to dogs.

Mat 15:27 And she *(the Gentile woman of Canaan)* said, Truth, Lord: yet the dogs eat of the crumbs which fall from their masters' table.

Mat 15:28 Then Jesus answered and said unto her *(the Gentile woman of Canaan)*, O woman, great *is* thy faith *(concerning My person; who I Am; and what I have authority to do, because My Father and the Holy Spirit are with me; and I do nothing except My Father agrees!)*: be it unto thee even as thou wilt *(or even as you have asked of me, be it unto you)*. And her daughter was made whole from that very hour *(And so, whenever anyone receives, and\ or declares (confesses) Jesus as their Lord and Master, the status of dog and of just being grass of the field, according to Isaiah 40:6 through 40:8 is rescinded! The Holy Spirit of God recreates them a "new creation in Jesus"; having access to every benefit unto eternal life from God through the Lord Jesus Christ; and even that of asking well being for loved ones, and others!).*

John 3 – Born Again:

Joh 3:1 There was a man of the Pharisees, named Nicodemus, a ruler of the Jews:

Joh 3:2 The same *(Nicodemus)* came to Jesus by night, and said unto him, Rabbi, we know that thou art a teacher come from God: for no man can do these miracles that thou doest, except God be with him.

Joh 3:3 Jesus answered and said unto him, Verily, verily, I say unto thee, Except a man be born again, he cannot see *(nor even perceive\ imagine?)* the kingdom of God.

Joh 3:4 Nicodemus saith unto him *(Jesus)*, How can a man be born when he is old? can he enter the second time into his mother's womb, and be born?

Joh 3:5 Jesus answered, Verily, verily, I say unto thee, Except a man be born of water *(physical, or natural birth?)* and of the Spirit *(the Holy Spirit make His abode\ presence with, and in you)*, he cannot enter into the kingdom of God.

Joh 3:6 That which is born of the flesh is flesh *(shall not enter the kingdom of God)*; and that which is born of the Spirit *(born again)* is spirit.

Joh 3:7 Marvel not that I said unto thee, Ye must be born again.

Joh 3:8 The wind *(a natural or physical example of the Holy Spirit!)* bloweth where it listeth *(or wants to)*, and thou hearest the sound thereof, but canst not tell whence it cometh, and whither it goeth: so is every one that is born of the Spirit *(or Holy Spirit of God). (But no one is born again (or born of the Spirit) except they ask and agree, or consent according to the Gospel and sacrifice of Jesus (it is not an automatic occurrence; Don't You See?) God does not override the will of anyone in this; remember John 3:16; John 14:6; Romans 10:9 and 10:10)! God wants you with Him, but it is according to your accepting Him.*

Anyone that is "born again" has (of necessity, present with them!) the Holy Spirit of God; Jesus sent Him to His followers on the Day of Pentecost!

Read Acts Chapter 2. If the Holy Spirit were not necessary Jesus would not have sent Him!?

However, one might ignore Him as so many do, and if you walk away from John 3:16/ John 14:6 (and the Judeo – Christian Word of God in general), the Holy Spirit <u>shall not</u> follow your leading! I am persuaded this would be somewhat akin to the action(s) of Judas walking away and betraying Jesus?

Joh 3:9 Nicodemus answered and said unto him *(Jesus)*, How can these things be?

Joh 3:10 Jesus answered and said unto him, Art thou a master *(or elder, and leader)* of Israel, and knowest not these things? *(The Lord Jesus considered this should have been known among the leadership of the Jews. But they simply had not received his witness (nor even that of Moses; see Deuteronomy 18:15 through 18:22!), and as a result, they did not know!)*

Joh 3:11 Verily, verily, I say unto thee, We *(God the Father; God the Son; God the Holy Spirit; and Moses)* speak that we do know, and testify that we have seen; and ye receive not our witness.

Joh 3:12 If I have told you earthly things, and ye believe not, how shall ye believe, if I tell you *of* heavenly things?

1Peter - Redeemed:

1Pe 1:17 And if ye call on the Father, who without respect of persons *(or whosoever will, may call)* judgeth according to every man's work, pass the time of your sojourning *(or temporary abode) here* in fear: *(the primary work of our sojourning is to believe on the Lord Jesus!)*

1Pe 1:18 Forasmuch as ye know that ye were not redeemed with corruptible things, *as* silver and gold, from your vain conversation *received* by tradition from your fathers;

1Pe 1:19 But with the precious blood *(sacrifice)* of Christ *(Jesus)*, as of a lamb without blemish and without spot *(or perfect sacrifice of God)*:

1Pe 1:20 Who verily was foreordained before the foundation of the world *(to be Kinsman Redeemer; the Sacrifice; the Atonement of human kind unto God; Savior of the world!)*, but was manifest in these last times *(or was not manifest until these end times)* for you,

1Pe 1:21 Who by him do believe in God, that raised him up from the dead, and gave him glory; that your faith and hope might be in God.

1Pe 1:22 Seeing ye have purified your souls in obeying the truth through the Spirit *(or by following the leading of the Holy Spirit)* unto unfeigned *(or sincere)* love of the brethren, see that ye love one another with a pure heart fervently:

1Pe 1:23 Being born again, not of corruptible seed, but of incorruptible, by the word of God, which liveth and abideth for ever.

1Pe 1:24 For all flesh *is* as grass, and all the glory of man as the flower of grass. The grass withereth, and the flower *(or beauty)* thereof falleth away:

1Pe 1:25 But the word of the Lord *(Jesus, which is now in you)* endureth for ever. And this is the word which by the gospel is preached unto you *(and without the word (or seed); the Lord Jesus Christ, no one shall continue!). (Refer to Isaiah 40:1 through 40:8)*!

Isaiah 40 – The grass of the field; not having been born again and redeemed, perishes forever:

The prophet Isaiah prophesy in Chapter 40 of the Biblical book which bear his name; that we: the human race, all of us, fit the category of grass of the field and the beauty of the flesh is as the flower of the grass. The Holy Spirit of God blows time upon the grass; the beauty *(or flower)* of the grass fades; the grass dies and wither, then is carried away of the wind, and it is no more, "forever"!

However, in that very same Chapter 40 of Isaiah, the prophet says: The God of Creation has provided the way of Jesus Christ *(whereby we may be born again, and therefore redeemed)*. Also by this we know from study this is the Father's sacrifice of His Son Jesus on the cross that surpasses every way of eternal loss to the human race, of them that believe. Let's just read a portion of what Isaiah Chapter 40 describes of this:

Isa 40:3 The voice of him *(or voice of John the Baptist heralded the appearing of Jesus)* that crieth *(or shout, announces)* in the wilderness, Prepare ye the way of the LORD *(Jesus)*, make straight in the desert a highway *(or the perfect way)* for our God *(Jesus)*.

Isa 40:4 Every valley shall be exalted, and every mountain and hill shall be made low *(because He is God, and because of His sacrifice)*: and the crooked shall be made straight, and the rough places plain *(or made smooth)*:

Isa 40:5 And the glory *(unimaginable power, wisdom, ability, mercy, grace, love)* of the LORD shall be revealed, and all flesh shall see *it* together: for the mouth of the LORD hath spoken *it*.

Isa 40:6 The voice said *(or the voice of the LORD said)*, Cry *(or shout)*. And he *(Isaiah the prophet)* said, What shall I cry/ *(or what shall I shout; announce)*? *(These next verses are what shall be shouted by the prophet!)* All flesh *is* grass, and all the goodliness *(or beauty)* thereof *is* as the flower of the field:

Isa 40:7 The grass withereth, the *(beauty of the)* flower fadeth: because the spirit *(Holy Spirit)* of the LORD bloweth *(time)* upon it *(or upon the grass and all things)*: surely the people *is* grass.

Isa 40:8 The grass withereth, the flower fadeth: but the word *(Jesus, the Son)* of our God shall stand *(or continue)* for ever. *And whosoever is in Him (or is of His seed) gets to continue forever, too!*

It is only in the Judeo – Christian Scriptures that Almighty God tells us over, and over, and over … what He is doing; what His plan is, "if you will"!

And Israel was commanded to declare the presence of Messiah, the Redeemer Christ Jesus at His appearing.

But today, we know only those like Apostle Paul; the other apostles; and followers that were in the immediate circle of Jesus obeyed the Holy Spirit, as follows:

Isa 40:9 O Zion, that bringest good tidings *(of Messiah\ Christ Jesus appearing)*, get thee up into the high mountain; O Jerusalem, that bringest good tidings, lift up thy voice with strength; lift *it* up, be not afraid; say unto the cities of Judah, Behold your God *(Son of God; the Lord Jesus Christ; Messiah; Redeemer: the Atonement…)*!

Isa 40:10 Behold, the Lord GOD will come with strong *hand (or exceeding great authority)*, and his arm *(the Son; the LORD Jesus)* shall rule for him *(the LORD God of Creation)*: behold, his reward *(salvation; offer of eternal life) is* with him *(Jesus)*, and his *(Sacrificial Atoning)* work before him.

Isa 40:11 He *(Jesus)* shall feed his flock *(followers, or believers)* like a shepherd: he shall gather the lambs with his arm, and carry *them* in his bosom, *and* shall gently lead those that are with young.

He is the Creator:

Isa 40:12 Who *(God; Son of God; Savior; Redeemer; Jesus)* hath measured the waters in the hollow of his hand, and meted out *(or spread out)* heaven with the span *(or from end to end)*, and comprehended *(or specified the amount of)* the dust of the earth in a measure, and weighed the mountains in scales, and the hills in a balance?

Isa 40:13 Who hath directed *(or instructed)* the Spirit of the LORD, or *being* his counsellor hath taught him *(the Holy Spirit of God)*?

Isa 40:14 With whom took he *(the Father; the LORD God of Creation)* counsel, and *who* instructed him, and taught him in the path of judgment, and taught him knowledge, and shewed to him the way of understanding?

Isa 40:15 Behold, the nations *are* as a drop *(of water)* of a bucket, and are counted as the small dust of the balance: behold, he taketh up the isles *(or far away places)* as a very little thing *(and no distance at all is too far away for Him)*.

Isa 40:16 And Lebanon *is* not sufficient *(or have enough wood)* to burn, nor the beasts thereof sufficient *(or plentiful enough)* for a burnt offering.

Isa 40:17 All nations before him *are* as nothing; and they are counted to him less than nothing, and vanity *(or excessive in self pride!)*.

Graven images and false gods are of no comparison with Him!

Isa 40:18 To whom then will ye liken God *(or the Son of God; the Lord Jesus Christ)*? or what likeness will ye compare unto him?

Isa 40:19 The workman melteth a graven image, and the goldsmith spreadeth it over with gold, and casteth silver chains. *(The rich man's false god is no comparison with Him)*

Isa 40:20 He that *is* so impoverished *(or poor)* that he hath no oblation *(or offering,)* chooseth a tree *that* will not rot; he seeketh unto *(search out)* him a cunning workman *(or craftsman)* to prepare *(fashion, or make)* a graven image, *that* shall not be moved. *(The poor man's false god is no comparison with Him)*

Don't You Know? And Have You Not Heard?

Isa 40:21 Have ye not known? have ye not heard? hath it not been told you from the beginning? have ye not understood from the foundations of the earth?

Isa 40:22 *It is* he *(the LORD God of Creation)* that sitteth upon the circle of the earth, and the inhabitants thereof *are* as grasshoppers; *(it is the LORD God of Creation)* that stretcheth out the heavens as a curtain, and spreadeth them out as a tent to dwell in:

Isa 40:23 *(It is the LORD God of Creation)* That bringeth the princes to nothing; he maketh the judges of the earth as vanity.

Isa 40:24 Yea, they *(judges of the earth)* shall not be planted *(or allowed to continue)*; yea, they shall not be sown: yea, their stock *(their product, or what they are proposing)* shall not take root in the earth: and he *(the Holy Spirit of God)* shall also blow *(time)* upon them, and they shall wither, and the whirlwind shall take them away as stubble.

Isa 40:25 To whom then will ye liken me, or shall I be equal? saith the Holy One *(of Israel, the LORD Jesus Christ!)*.

Isa 40:26 Lift up your eyes on high, and behold who hath created these *things,* that bringeth out their host by number: he calleth them all by names by the greatness of his might, for that *he is* strong in power; not one faileth *(the purpose God intended)*.

Why do you think your ways are beyond or better than those of the LORD God of Creation?

Isa 40:27 Why sayest thou, O Jacob *(or sons of Jacob)*, and speakest, O Israel, *(that)* My way is hid from *(or is unknown to)* the LORD *(God)*, and my judgment is passed over from *(or above that of)* my God? *(Why do you say this is the twenty first (21ˢᵗ) century; God is out dated, or God needs help with His program, let us show Him how things really are!*

Isa 40:28 Hast thou not known? hast thou not heard, *that* the everlasting God, the LORD, the Creator of the ends of the earth, fainteth not, neither is weary? *there is* no searching *(unto exhausting)* of his understanding.

Isa 40:29 He giveth power to the faint; and to *them that have* no might he increaseth strength.

Isa 40:30 Even the youths *(or those of great stamina)* shall faint and be weary, and the young men shall utterly fall:

Isa 40:31 But they that wait upon the LORD *(of Creation)* shall renew *their* strength; they shall mount up with wings as eagles; they shall run, and not be weary; *and* they shall walk, and not faint.

But if we do not come to <u>the place</u> of believing and obeying it (His Word(s)/ His plan/ His Son Jesus), we shall die as the grass of the field, and never know life again for ever and ever, <u>just as the dog</u>!

So what is holding the world back, and/ or getting in its way: Is It Unbelief Because Of PRIDE, or PRIDE, Because of Unbelief? And just what do you suppose pride shall get anyone on their last day of this natural life?

But faith in the Gospel and our Lord Jesus Christ *(the sacrifice of Christ Jesus on the cross)* brings benefits not yet fully known; Hallelujah, Hallelujah, Hallelujah, and Amen!

RETURN LORD JESUS!

First Kings of Israel - At the time of events beginning in *1 Samuel* it had not yet been five hundred *(500)* years since the LORD God spoke to Moses out of the burning bush on Mount Sinai; Arabia *(of Old Testament Midian)*. *This date approximation "of 500 years" is given with reference to 1 Kings 6:1, which states the following:*

1Ki 6:1 And it came to pass in the four hundred and eightieth *(480th)* year after the children of Israel were come out of the land of Egypt *(which was about 1500 B.C.)*, in the fourth *(4th)* year of Solomon's reign over Israel, in the month Zif, which *is* the second *(2nd)* month, that he *(Solomon)* began to build the house *(or Temple)* of the LORD *(this would have been about (1020 B.C.), or 1500 B.C. – 480 B.C. = 1020 B.C.; the (4th) year of Solomon's reign.*

David ruled for forty (40) years before Solomon (2 Samuel 5:4 and 5:5), and Saul ruled for about forty (40) years before David (Acts 13:31). Thus, a more accurate estimate of the time period of Judges would be (1500 B.C. – ((40 + 40 + 4) + (1020 B.C.)) – (the approximate fifty (50) years, or so, of Moses and Joshua's leadership)) = 346 years! And the events of 1 Samuel would have begun about 1104 B.C., or 1020 B.C. + (40 + 40 + 4) = 1104 B.C. The beginning of David's reign was about (1020 + 40 + 4) = 1064 B.C.!

Since Solomon also ruled 40 years (1 Kings 11:42), his reign ended about 984 B.C., or (1020 B.C. – 36 = 984 B.C.).

Heathen – *I am persuaded the meaning of this word has no real use and/ or value unless it is viewed from the eyes of the Real and True God of Creation! Any other view has no lasting impact and meaning, because it shall die forever with the person, or persons view point; especially if the True Creator's evaluation is not accepted, and embraced. And so, the "heathen" in the sight of the True God and Creator is anyone that does not have Him (God) in their life and living!*

But from the perspective of souls that do not believe there is a One True God, or erroneously believe that their particular deity is God the following meaning may be applied:

Heathen people(s) collectively, and especially (in the use of one's "holy book") are those who did not (or does not) worship the God of their fathers: Where the God of Israel is concerned, this would be the God of the Judeo – Christian Bible; which God is also the God of Abraham, Isaac, and Jacob.

And so, everyone today has available this dilemma (<u>whether they think it important or not</u>) of giving consideration to the offering of <u>Jesus the Messiah and Christ</u>, according to John 3:16, as described in the Judeo – Christian Holy Bible Books. The other choices are to follow after anything else contrary to the Judeo – Christian Doctrine!

Thus, everyone chooses; and the Judeo – Christine Scriptures makes the following clear: Whosoever will believe the Gospel of Jesus Christ "SHALL" be saved, and enter life that is eternal with the True God of Creation, and Jesus Christ! Amen.

Israel Today – There is much disagreement in present day conversation concerning which portions of land(s) Israel is not entitled to occupy. According to Zechariah Chapter 14, and other Judeo – Christian passages of scripture, the Lord Jesus Christ shall settle every disagreement upon His return, and second coming! This map image below provides a view of Israel among her many friends, neighbors, and enemies?

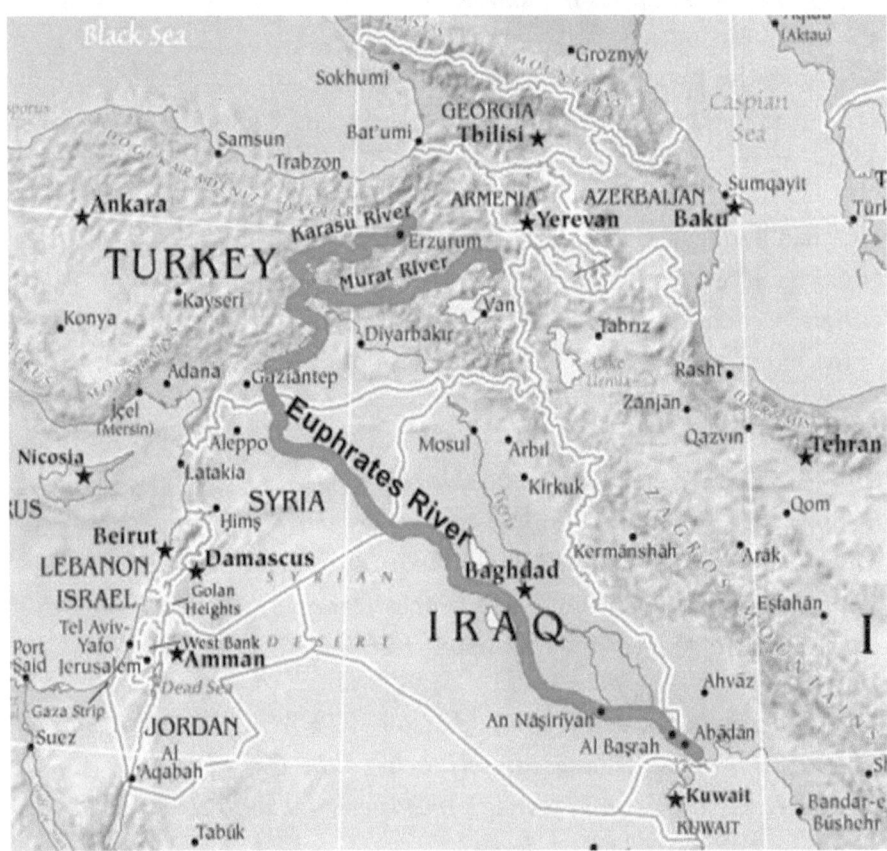

Job Chapters 40 and 41

Job Chapter 40

Moreover the LORD answered Job, and said,
Shall he that contendeth with the Almighty instruct *him?* he that reproveth *(disapprove of)* God, let him answer it.
Then Job answered the LORD, and said,

Job 40:1 through 40:3

Job acknowledges his unworthiness before the presence of the LORD God:

Behold, I am vile *(of little worth or value)*; what shall I answer thee? I will lay mine hand upon my mouth.
Once have I spoken; but I will not answer: yea, twice; but I will proceed no further.

Job 40:4 and 40:5

The LORD God continues answering Job:
Then answered the LORD unto Job out of the whirlwind, and said,

Gird up thy loins now like a man: I will demand of thee, and declare thou unto me.
Wilt thou also disannul my judgment *(or my declaration of right)*? wilt thou condemn me, that thou mayest be righteous?
Hast thou an arm *(authority, might, power)* like God? or canst thou thunder with a voice like him *(the LORD God)*?
Deck thyself now *with* majesty and excellency; and array thyself with glory and beauty.
Cast abroad the rage of thy wrath: and behold every one *that is* proud, and abase him.
Look on every one *that is* proud, *and* bring him low; and tread down the wicked in their place.
Hide them in the dust together; *and* bind their faces in secret.
Then will I also confess unto thee that thine own right hand can save thee.

Job 40:6 through 40:14

The LORD God made the behemoth, which Job 40:15 through 40:24 describes. The description seems to fit that of many species of dinosaur we are taught about, according to fossil record today. But in no way does the description resemble that of an elephant; the largest living land animal we know exists today. Refer to "Behemoth" in "Definitions & Figures":

Behold now behemoth *(huge, or monstrous land creature)*, which I *(the LORD God)* made with *(or along side)* thee; he eateth grass as an ox.

Lo now, his strength *is* in his loins, and his force *(or center of his body weight?)* *is* in the navel of his belly.

He moveth his tail like a cedar: the sinews *(or skin, muscle, bone?)* of his stones *(or armor like scales?)* are wrapped together.

His bones *are as* strong pieces of brass; his bones *are* like bars of iron.

He *is* the chief of the ways of God: he *(God)* that made him can make his sword to approach *(or penetrate?)* unto him.

Surely the mountains *(are required to)* bring him forth food *(in other words he consumes unbelievable quantities of plant food!)*, where all the beasts of the field play.

He lieth under the shady trees, in the covert *(or enclosed parts)* of the reed *(or tall plants with leaves)*, and fens *(or marshy, flooded land of plants)*.

The shady trees cover him *with* their shadow; the willows of the brook compass him about.

Behold, he drinketh up a river, *and* hasteth not *(or without hurrying)*: he trusteth that he can draw up Jordan into his mouth.

He taketh it with his eyes: *his* nose pierceth through snares *(this seem to be saying the behemoth has a excellent sense of vision and smell)*.

Job 40:15 through 40:24

Job Chapter 41

The LORD God made the leviathan, which Job 41:1 through 41:34 seems to be describing as a dragon (a meat eater?), though to be an "ancient myth" today. The fact that it is a sea dwelling creature (or perhaps inhabit the sea most of its existence, and dies there?) may explain why no fossil record has been uncovered or seen! The description is not that of a smooth skinned whale; the largest living sea creature we know exists today. Refer to "Leviathan" in "Definitions & Figures":

Canst thou draw out leviathan *(a very large sea creature)* with an hook? or his tongue with a cord *(or fishing line)* which thou lettest down?
Canst thou put an hook into his nose? or bore his jaw through with a thorn?
Will he make many supplications unto thee? will he speak soft *words* unto thee?
Will he make a covenant with thee? wilt thou take him for a servant for ever?
Wilt thou play with him as *with* a bird? or wilt thou bind him for thy maidens *(for entertainment as a pet)*?
Shall the companions *(or sellers of merchandise?)* make a banquet of him? shall they part *(or divide)* him among the merchants *(to be sold)*?
Canst thou fill his skin with barbed irons? or his head with fish spears *(this may imply that leviathan's skin protrude iron barbs, and his head spear like rods! And the question is, "can you put those things in him?")*?
Lay thine hand upon him, remember the battle *(does this mean touching leviathan would remind one of instruments used in battle?)*, do no more *(or do no more than touch him, lest you cause him to stir)*.
Behold, the hope of him is in vain *(does this mean leviathan was becoming extinct, or was already extinct? No one has encountered any today, and live to talk about it!)*: shall not *one* be cast down even at the sight of him *(in other words he is scary to look at)*?
None *is so* fierce that dare stir him up: who then is able to stand before me *(LORD God of Creation that made him)*?

Who hath prevented *(or **withstood**)* me *(to success)*, that I should repay him? *whatsoever is* under the whole heaven is mine.

I will not conceal *(hide)* his *(leviathan's)* parts, nor his power, nor his comely *(agreeable or less scary)* proportion.

Who can discover the face of his garment? *or* who can come *to him* with his double bridle *(in other words who can tame him, as one would tame a horse)*?

Who can open the doors *(or mouth)* of his face? his teeth *are* terrible *(or frightening)* round about.

His scales *are his* pride, shut up together *as with* a close seal *(like water proof)*.

One *(his scale)* is so near to another, that no air can come between them.

They are joined one to another, they stick together, that they cannot be sundered *(or separated)*.

By his neesings *(or **sneezing?**)* a light doth shine, and his eyes *are* like the eyelids of the morning *(not fully opened?)*.

Out of his mouth go burning lamps *(or **burning chunks of hot air?**)*, and sparks of fire leap out.

Out of his nostrils goeth smoke, as *out* of a seething *(or **boiling**)* pot or caldron.

His breath kindleth coals, and a flame goeth out of his mouth.

In his neck remaineth strength, and sorrow is turned into joy before him.

The flakes of his flesh are joined together: they are firm in themselves; they cannot be moved.

His heart is as firm as a stone; yea, as hard as a piece of the nether *millstone*.

When he raiseth up himself, the mighty are afraid: by reason of breakings they purify themselves *(or **they relieve themselves of bodily waste?**)*.

The sword of him that layeth at him cannot hold: the spear, the dart, nor the habergeon *(or **nothing manmade can penetrate his scale of armor**)*.

He esteemeth *(or **regard**)* iron as straw, *and* brass as rotten wood.

The arrow cannot make him flee: slingstones are turned with him into stubble.

Darts are counted as stubble: he laugheth at the shaking of a spear.

Sharp stones *are* under him *(or protect his under side)*: he spreadeth *(or shed)* sharp pointed things upon the mire *(or mud where he has rested?)*.

He maketh the deep to boil like a pot: he maketh the sea like a pot of ointment *(or he leaves a distinct odor behind?)*.

He maketh a path to shine after him; *one* would think the deep *to be* hoary *(gray or white with age?)*.

Upon earth there is not his like, who is made without fear.

He beholdeth all high *things:* he *is* a king over all the children of pride.

Job 41:1 through 41:34

Judges – After the leadership of Joshua, the LORD God did not promote another leader for Israel immediately; thus, no central government structure existed as with the leaderships of Moses and Joshua! But when the people fell hopelessly away from God into false god and idol worship *(as Moses warned against in final Chapters of Deuteronomy)*; and became oppressed by the spoiler, and subjects of the heathen enemies round about, the LORD God would send the Holy Spirit upon someone of His choosing! It would then become obvious that God had chosen the person to "Judge Israel" by the exploits, and/or wisdom that resulted of their actions!

"Judge" was the name given to those individuals that presided over the affairs of the Israelites during the interval from the death of Joshua until Saul who became the first king in Israel *(Judges 2:18)*. This period was a time of Israel's "general and almost wholesale" failure to obey commandments the LORD God had given by Moses, which the people promised to obey by covenant.

A person in the office of judges continued, as judge, unto the end of his life, but the office was not hereditary, neither could the judge appoint a successor.

Their authority was suppose to be according to the law alone, but in those days there was no king, and every man did that which was right in his own eyes *(Judges 17:6, 18:1, 19:1, and 21:25)*! We see this attitude, and its destructive results portrayed with Abimelech in *Judges Chapter 9*, declaring himself king, and killing his other brothers; all sons of Gideon. Another, even more deadly consequence of this kind of lawlessness is recorded in the final three *(3) Chapter; Judges 19, 20, and 21*!

And yet, the record shows, during the conflict of all the other tribes against Benjamin, that they consulted the divine King *(the LORD God)* through Phinehas, the son of Eleazar, the son of Aaron *(Judges 20:25 through 20:28)*. This imply that the functionality of Urim and

Thummim had not been lost at this time *(Deuteronomy 16:18 through 16:22; Deuteronomy 17:8 through 17:13, and Numbers 27:21).*

The judge's authority extended primarily over those tribes by whom they had been elected or acknowledged. There was no monetary reward attached to their office, and they bore no external indication of special consideration.

Obvious cases of direct divine appointment are those of Gideon and Samson. And Samson was in the unique position of having been identified from before his birth; ordained "to begin to deliver Israel".

Deborah was a prophetess used to deliver Israel, but had already been serving as a judge, when she appointed Barak the son of Abinoam out of Kedesh Naphtali to destroy the armies of king Jabin *(Judges Chapter 2).*

The time of judges ended with Samuel, whom the LORD God called to be a prophet!

Shiloh – "Shiloh"; a place of rest, a city of Ephraim *(which Ephraim, is also the family inheritance for Joshua)*, "on the north side of Bethel," from which it is a distant of about ten *(10)* miles *(Judges 21:19)*; the modern Seilun (the Arabic for Shiloh), a "mass of shapeless ruins". Here, centuries earlier Joshua set up the tabernacle after crossing over Jordan *(Joshua 18:1 through 18:10)*, where it remained during all the period of the Book of Judges till the Ark of the Testimony fell into the hands of the Philistines. "It seems no spot in ancient Israel could be more secluded than this early sanctuary Joshua and the children of Israel set up; nothing more featureless than the landscape around; so featureless, indeed, the landscape and so secluded the spot that from the time of Jeremiah the prophet till its re-discovery by Dr. Robinson in 1838 the very site was forgotten and unknown". It is referred to by *(Jeremiah 7:12 through 7:14)*; and *(Jeremiah 26:4 through 26:9)* five hundred *(500)* years after its destruction *(which occurred about the time Eli and his sons were priests in Israel: 1 Samuel Chapter 4)*. Also refer to *Psalms 78:60!*

Solomon's Temple – This figure is a general illustration of what the Temple that replaced the Tabernacle of Moses may have looked.

Four hundred and eighty *(480)* year after the children of Israel were come out of the land of Egypt, in the fourth *(4ᵗʰ)* year of Solomon's reign over Israel, in the month Zif, which *is* the second *(2ⁿᵈ)* month *(of the Israeli year)*, Solomon began to build the house of the LORD.

Temple Illustration – An illustration of the approximate configuration *(floor plan)* of Solomon's Temple:

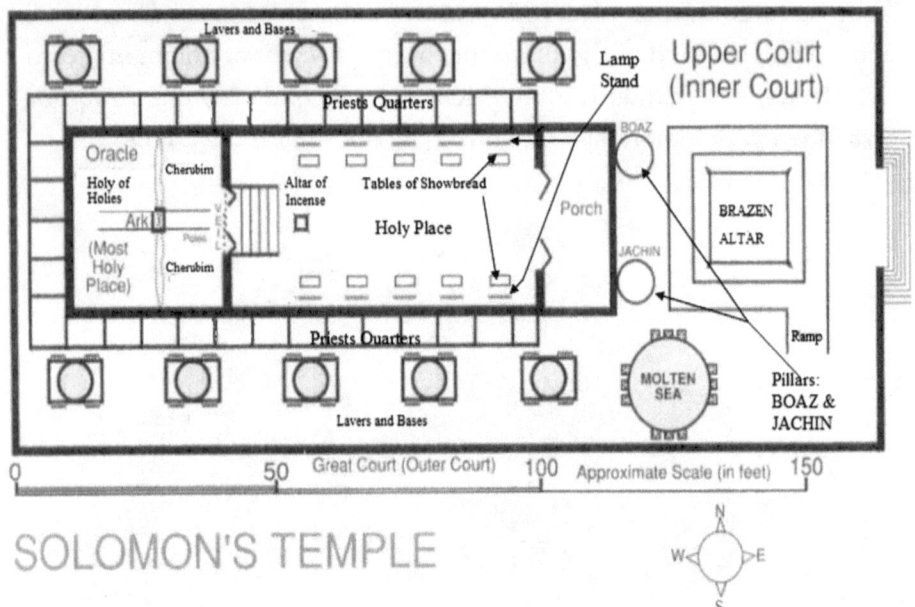

SOLOMON'S TEMPLE

The Kinsman Redeemer – The LORD God instructed Moses to implement the principle describing the "Kinsman Redeemer" into the law and commandments to Israel.

This speaks of one having much seeing his kinsman with little, or no means to help himself, even to the extent of not having what is needed to continue day to day living. And the kinsman with much *"choose as his responsibility"* to meet the redeeming needs of his kinsman *(See Deuteronomy Chapter 15)*!

The primary message of the Book of Ruth describes the Kinsman Redeemer through the relationship of Boaz and Ruth.

Obviously Boaz, the kinsman redeemer of Ruth is a type of the Lord Jesus Christ not only redeeming Israel at His first visitation in the world, but Jesus is the ultimate Kinsman Redeemer that redeems "whosoever will" unto the Father according to *John 3:16!*

Recall what the LORD God instructed Moses to write in Genesis 1:26 and 1:27:

Gen 1:26 And God said, Let us make man in our image, after our likeness: and let them have dominion over the fish of the sea, and over the fowl of the air, and over the cattle, and over all the earth, and over every creeping thing that creepeth upon the earth.
Gen 1:27 So God created man in his *own* image, in the image of God created he him; male and female created he them.

Bible researchers speculate this occurred about Six Thousand Two Hundred (6200) Years Ago: The Creation of Adam (Man in the image of God; never done before!? Thus, man is created one hundred (100) percent man, and akin to God!?)

But then Physical Life continued, without Life of the Spirit after the man, Adam sinned against God in disobedience– Genesis Chapter 3 forward …

And so, relationship between God and man can be made right again; but only if there is a "Kinsman Redeemer" to complete the redemption!

In my mind the implication here spawns several questions as follows:

- There is no missing link between <u>*any*</u> prehistory creature and this man, Adam that is akin to God; <u>*and therefore redeemable (or can be brought back!)*</u>? Thus, the dog is not redeemable; there can be another one, but not the same one, ever! And so, any person *rejecting John 3:16 (although redeemable)* achieve the unredeemable state as the dog? And the finality of their living shall be that of grass in the field, as described by Isaiah Chapter 40:6 through 40:8!

Mat 7:6 Give not that which is holy unto the dogs, neither cast ye your pearls before swine, lest they trample them under their feet, and turn again and rend you.

Mat 15:26 But he answered and said, It is not meet to take the children's bread, and to cast *it* to dogs.

Mat 15:27 And she said, Truth, Lord: yet the dogs eat of the crumbs which fall from their masters' table.

- *The Holy Spirit of God commanded manifestation of God the Son, Jesus in the flesh, whereby the fallen may become redeemed Son of Adam; and therefore akin to God? Thus, Jesus had to be (of necessity); one hundred (100) percent man, and one hundred (100) percent God?*
- No one shall ever compile a list of all the attributes of the Eternal Almighty God whereby it may be determined, how much of Himself God put in Adam, and therefore the human race?

1Jn 3:2 Beloved, now are we the sons of God, and it doth not yet appear what we shall be: but we know that, when he shall appear, we shall be like him; for we shall see him as he is.

- Is there anything too hard for the LORD, or is there anything impossible with the LORD God?

Jer 32:17 Ah Lord GOD! behold, thou hast made the heaven and the earth by thy great power and stretched out arm, *and* there is nothing too hard for thee:

Jer 32:27 Behold, I *am* the LORD, the God of all flesh: is there any thing too hard for me?

Mat 19:26 But Jesus beheld *them,* and said unto them, With men this is impossible; but with God all things are possible.

Mar 9:23 Jesus said unto him, If thou canst believe, all things *are* possible to him that believeth.

Mar 10:27 And Jesus looking upon them saith, With men *it is* impossible, but not with God: for with God all things are possible.

Mar_14:36 And he said, Abba, Father, all things *are* possible unto thee; take away this cup from me: nevertheless not what I will, but what thou wilt.

Thy Throne Forever – The eternal LORD and God of Creation made this promise of his eternal kingdom to King David. But New Testament Judeo – Christian Scriptures clearly explains that corruptible can not inherit incorruptible **(1 Corinthians 15:53 through 15:55)**, because incorruptible is *"forever"*. Thus, the obvious and natural question arises; "how is this promise the LORD God gave corruptible David, possible"?

Throughout history no throne of man has continued more than a hand full of years, compared to all the time of recorded history; and the promise to David was for eternity! And so, the short answer to the question is, *"by love; grace; mercy; regeneration\ resurrection; inheritance; Kinsman Redemption; sacrifice; and ... other works of the*

Lord Jesus Christ (Son of God 100%; son, and progeny of King David, who is 100% man)"!

The genealogy of the Lord Jesus Christ is given in the New Testament Book of Matthew Chapter 1(one). And we see that his genealogy traces through David, the Great King of Israel; the youngest son of Jesse, as is revealed in scriptures of Ruth Chapter 4, 1 Samuel Chapter 16, and 2 Samuel Chapter 7. Thus, the flesh and blood man Jesus, Messiah traces unto the man, Adam (no demonic hybrid, of any sorts was given, and can not claim, such a genealogy); and he, the man Adam was created of God in the image of God! Study again, Genesis 1:26 and 1:27 and John 10:1 through 10:18. Thus, the genealogy is proven, according to the Word of God; without sin or contamination of any sort!

But to see the complete *(or full)* answer of sacrificing, atoning and inheritance *(of the LORD God; Jesus the Son, for his followers and believers)* we must "diligently" study both, the Old and New Testament Judeo – Christian Bible Books; which is *the Words of God given to us that we may know Him and His plans for the human race; no other document(s) provide this!* Do we not see in this how the LORD God of Creation leaves nothing to chance; and who else would you suppose could maintain such precise and factual records of the centuries?

Gen 18:14 Is any thing too hard for the LORD? At the time appointed I will return unto thee, according to the time of life, and Sarah *(at 90 years of age)* shall have a son *(Isaac)*.

Jer 32:17 Ah Lord GOD! behold, thou hast made the heaven and the earth by thy great power and stretched out arm, *and* there is nothing too hard for thee:

Jer 32:27 Behold, I *am* the LORD, the God of all flesh: is there any thing too hard for me?

Mat 19:26 But Jesus beheld *them*, and said unto them, With men this is impossible; but with God all things are possible.

Mar 9:23 Jesus said unto him, If thou canst believe, all things *are* possible to him that believeth.

Mar 10:27 And Jesus looking upon them saith, With men *it is* impossible, but not with God: for with God all things are possible.

Thus, the eternal LORD and God of Creation establish the final state of those BELIEVERS in Him to be eternally with God!

Urim and the Thummim, or Thummim and the Urim – The Urim and the Thummim is associated with the functionality of the high priest's ephod for discerning the will of God for the children of Israel without the presence of Moses.

The LORD God consistently spoke with Moses of what He wanted done concerning Israel, and we see in ***Exodus Chapter 19*** that the LORD wanted this same relationship with the elders of every tribe. But the people's disobedience and unbelief hindered God from approaching them as He did with Moses, because it would result in their death!

Thus, the LORD God gave Moses instruction for the Leviticus Priesthood whereby the high priest *(among his duties)* could determine the will of God for the people without being in direct conversation with God. Thus, the ephod with the breastplate, and "the Urim and the Thummim" provided this function *(refer to Exodus 28:1 through 28:30)*.

Scripture does not give details of how the high priest was to navigate the Urim and the Thummim for a reliable conclusion about the will of God, but I am persuaded God did not provide Moses with something that was useless! The final details of instructions were no doubt passed on by word of mouth from Moses to Aaron first, and then from high priest to high priest thereafter, until the time of Eli the high priest *(1 Samuel Chapter 4)*, and Samuel (the last Judge and first **prophet;** *1 Samuel 25:1, and 15:1, 1 Samuel Chapter 3)*?

PREVIOUS WRITINGS

- King James Version of the Bible
- Author's Previously Published Works
  - A Testimony of Jesus; Messiah, Son of the Living God. Published, Dec. 30, 2013:
    http://www.amazon.com/s/ref=nb_sb_noss?url=search-alias%3Daps&field-keywords=Jimmie+Jennings&rh=i%3Aaps%2Ck%3AJimmie+Jennings

  - Separation From God Has NO Victory; But the Invitation of John 3:16 Remains, July 2014:

  - Gog Magog, and Armageddon; Origins of End Time Battles, Men; and Judgments of God, April 2014:

  - A Testimony of Jesus 2; His Abundant Love, Work, and Prophecy, Sept 2014:

  - A Study of John's Revelation; End of Kingdoms Ruled by Men, Sept 2014:

  - A Testimony of Jesus 3: Jesus in the Pages of Genesis, March 2015:

  - A Testimony of Jesus 4: Jesus and His Disciples (Harvesting Fields 1), June 2015:

  - A Testimony of Jesus 5: Jesus and His Disciples (Harvesting Fields 2), June 2015:

- A Testimony of Jesus 6: O Jerusalem, Jerusalem (Jeremiah in Perils), August 2015:

- A Testimony of Jesus 7: O Jerusalem, Jerusalem (Daniel; Visions and Dreams), September 2015:

- A Testimony of Jesus 8: O Jerusalem, Jerusalem (Ezekiel's; Visions), January 2016:

- A Testimony of Jesus 9: The Word of God for every Creature, March 2016:

- A Testimony of Jesus 10: Judah after Babylonian Exile End, April 2016:

- A Testimony of Jesus 11: God Called and Used Moses Mightily (Exodus), June 2016:

- A Testimony of Jesus 12: God Called and Used Moses Mightily (The Mosaic Law & Levi), September 2016:

- A Testimony of Jesus 13: God Called and Used Moses Mightily (Moses Number' Israel), November 2016:

- A Testimony of Jesus 14: God Called and Used Moses Mightily (Deuteronomy), March 2017:

- A Testimony of Jesus 15: God Called and Used JOSHUA to Walk After Moses, April 2017:

- A Testimony of Jesus 16: Jesus among the Pages of Job, April 2017:

- A Testimony of Jesus 17: Evaluating Israel: The Books of Judges and Ruth, June 2017:

- A Testimony of Jesus 18: 1 & 2 Samuel (Thy Throne Forever I), September 2017:

- A Testimony of Jesus: 1 & 2 Kings (Thy Throne Forever II), April 2018:

- A Timeline & Testimony of Jesus (Thy Throne Forever III), May 2018:

- ISAIAH & A Testimony of Jesus (Thy Throne Forever IV), June 2018:

- A Testimony of Jesus: with the Holy Spirit (Thy Throne Forever V), July 2018:

- 1 & 2 Chronicles & A Testimony of Jesus (Thy Throne Forever VI), August 2018:

- Prophetic RECORDS & A Testimony of Jesus (Thy Throne Forever VII), November 2018:
https://www.amazon.com/gp/offer-listing/1729637302/ref=sr_1_31_olp?s=books&ie=UTF8&qid=1547690643&sr=1-31&keywords=jimmie+jennings

- A Testimony of Jesus, His Purpose His Invitation (Thy Throne Forever VIII), January 2019:
https://www.amazon.com/Testimony-Jesus-Purpose-Invitation-Forever/dp/1795152109/ref=sr_1_1?keywords=jimmie+jennings&qid=1564526212&s=books&sr=1-1

- A Testimony of Jesus, The Witness the Task and Transfiguration, August 2019:

https://www.amazon.com/dp/1086839463/ref=sr_1_1?keywords=jimmie+jennings&qid=1565267458&s=books&sr=1-1

- A Testimony of Jesus, THE PSALMS, August 2019: https://www.amazon.com/Testimony-Jesus-PSALMS-Jimmie-Jennings/dp/1089349114/ref=sr_1_3?keywords=Jimmie+Jennings&qid=1565725197&s=gateway&sr=8-3

- My Website – www.jkejennings-author.com
- Specific articles on My Website
  - Where is Mount Sinai Really
  - Revelation Against Error III
  - Stoned for Mysteries of Jesus
  - Blasphemy of the Holy Spirit
  - LORD God Not Done With Israel
  - Answering ECCLESASTES' Vanity
  - Creation Has Cycles of Event_PRT2
  - Kingdom of Heaven Material
  - Others, take a look!

www.ingramcontent.com/pod-product-compliance
Lightning Source LLC
Chambersburg PA
CBHW030327100526
44592CB00010B/596